UNDERNEATH IT ALL

POST GRADUATE LEVEL REVELATIONS LIFT ADMINISTRATIVE ASSISTANTS TO NEW HEIGHTS

D0062080

JOAN BURGE

Underneath It All © 2009 Joan Burge

Publishing by
INSIGHT PUBLISHING
647 Wall Street
Sevierville, Tennessee 37862

10 9 8 7 6 5 4 3 2 1

ISBN 978-1-60013-307-7

TABLE OF CONTENTS

ACKNOWLEDGEMENTS

Wow! I don't know how to begin paying tribute to all the wonderful people I want to acknowledge who were a part of the undertakings of this book and were my support network during the past year. I will try to do my best and hope that I have left no one out.

I want to start by thanking my incredible Chief Executive Assistant, Jasmine Freeman. Jasmine is not only a great assistant, but a wonderful person. She has more than stepped up to the plate in the short two years she has been with me. As you read Chapter 6, The Anatomy of a Strategic Partnership – Jasmine and I have nailed it! A large part of that is due to Jasmine embracing everything that has come her way, committing to excellence, and desiring a work partnership.

Fortunately, we have a great team at Office Dynamics so thanks to all our staff especially Jamie, Dave, Sharyn, Lisa and Kathy.

As in my last book, *Become an Inner Circle Assistant*, the stories and illustrations you read are those of real people I've encountered, trained, or coached. One benefit of my work is that I get to meet thousands of executives, managers, administrative assistants, executive assistants, and support people in every type of industry and size business. I learn as much from them as they learn from me. They are a great blessing in my life!

Marilyn Pincus, once again, has been a critical player in the birth of this book. I thank her for the Prelude she wrote because I could not do it myself or as eloquently as she expressed.

Most importantly, I want to express my profound appreciation to my parents, sisters, aunts, uncles, cousins, nieces, nephews, relatives, neighbors, and dear friends who have been by my side for the past 16 months. I never thought I would get to where I am today—I didn't even want to write this book. While 90% of them do not live in Nevada, we are as close as can be thanks to technology and blogs!

Last but not least, thanks to all my clients, business support networks, colleagues, and vendors.

DEDICATION

First and foremost, this book is dedicated to my wonderful husband, Dave, who has been a pillar of strength through his battle with pancreatic cancer; someone who is an intelligent business person, dedicated life partner, and my best friend.

This is also dedicated to my wonderful grandchildren, Bradley, Eian, and Madison; my supportive adult children, Lauren, Brian, and Wade. May they always remember that while life is not always fair, God is always good and He will bring you through anything.

I am dedicating 10% of all book sales to the Pancreatic Cancer Action Network in honor of all the patients and their family members who have experienced the effects of this disease.

FOREWORD

As the Chief Executive Assistant to John Chambers, Chairman and CEO of Cisco Systems, I thought I was finally performing at the top administrative skill level and at the pinnacle of my profession having worked with John in this role for over 17 years. Then I met Joan Burge, author of *Become An Inner Circle Assistant*, creator of the Star Achievement Administrative and Manager Training program and CEO of her own company, Office Dynamics. Her insights showed me that the administrative role has completely changed and that we are performing on an entirely new playing field. John Chambers has stated many times, *"When I was looking for an assistant, what people didn't understand is that I was not looking for a senior secretary, I was looking for a true business partner, someone who makes it a point to know the business, what my priorities are and who could represent me as well as the organization in the absolute best professional light."* These are definitely the "new" skills that are required in today's working environment.

In her new book *Underneath It All*, her insights in to what it will take in the "new world" of the Administrative Professional are right on! Administrators will need an entirely new set of skills such as a commitment to quality performance, cognitive thinking and management of organizational goals. This book will show them how they can become masters of their career and earn a seat at the executive table.

Joan brings in to the light from the depths of business, the true value that the administrative professional has in terms of her or his relationship with their principals, their organizations and the companies that they work for. I have met many "experts" who think they have a good view of the administrative world and what it takes to be successful, however, none have actually been in the role to know the true nature of this profession. Joan Burge truly speaks from experience when she shares her philosophies and her stories. And because she has been an Executive Assistant herself, an instructor and the CEO of her own company, she brings a wealth of knowledge from both sides of the desk. Her recent challenging personal and professional journey was the catalyst for her to write this book. The pages contained within this book chart the way for all administrators who are aspiring to a fulfilling career. I consider this book a "must read" for every administrative professional and manager who wants to rise above the average and be seen and heard in business.

Debbie Gross
Chief Executive Assistant to John Chambers
Chairman & CEO Cisco Systems, Inc.

A Prelude

This book could not have been written at an earlier date.

Is it because ….
- of world events? NO
- the role of the *Admin* has changed markedly? NO
- more *Admins* are ready for more information? THAT MAY BE TRUE but -- it's not the whole story.

The answer isn't complicated. The revelations, however, are profound!

AT AN EARLIER DATE THE FOLLOWING HAD NOT OCCURRED.

During the past three years, the author has ventured into new worlds. She has gone kicking and screaming onto new playing fields. She would never agree to visit these places but, no one gave her a choice. Joan Burge has been a visionary for administrative training and development since 1990. She is the author of other books; most notably, BECOME AN INNER CIRCLE ASSISTANT. But this book, UNDERNEATH IT ALL is different because Joan is different. Suffice it to say, Joan has met the enemy and its name is: mortality. She has been immersed in the fight her husband of 31 years wages against pancreatic cancer. As a successful entrepreneur she is accustomed to being in-charge. As a one-time highly appreciated Admin herself, she knows how effective finely honed skills are … *let me learn how to do it and I'll do it.* Well, she is not in-charge. She can not learn what has not yet been discovered. She can not do what is undoable. In the process of finding ways to cope – ANOTHER DIMENSION has been revealed to Joan. She "sees" how it relates to everything! This is why UNDERNEATH IT ALL is a book whose time has come. You're about to explore key points with Joan that lead to success and you're likely to wonder *who switched on the lights?* Once you "see" what is *underneath it all*, you will become a more effective person. In short, you will not become a more effective Admin. You will not become a more effective Mother. You will not become a more effective Life Partner. You will become a more effective Admin, Mother and Life Partner.

While *life was happening* around her (e.g., her own major surgery, her beloved father's unexpected hospital confinement in another state and other once-in-a-lifetime personal challenges), Joan's work also produced three years of solid research which concluded: 90% of the requirements for being a successful Admin revolve around the soft skills … 10% revolve around technology and technical skills. Three years ago, this was virtually unknown but that's not all …

On the final pages of UNDERNEATH IT ALL you'll find the *Curtain Going Up On Things To Come* which spotlights something Joan calls *Admins' DNA.*

In the world of biology, DNA refers to deoxyribonucleic acid. It is the molecule that encodes genetic information. (Source: www.biology-online.org/dictionary/Dna.)

What does that have to do with *Admins?*

Joan has identified "what it takes to be the best in this profession."

Not everyone who aspires to be an assistant is well "encoded" to succeed.

That's quite a revelation coming from a woman who is an eternal optimist, a dynamic motivator and a tireless proponent of encouragement.

THE FORMULA FACTOR

While life was happening … one client asked "Is there a formula you have discovered; traits that would be critical for working with a CEO? In other words, if I'm interviewing what are the traits I should be looking for that you have identified as important and critical to success?" It was a good question and Joan thought about how to answer it as she was revising a segment of her World Class Assistant workshop.

She removed something old and asked herself what to add. What's new? What's different? The answer popped … "DNA is what we're made of and YES … there is DNA for a Star Assistant!"

"I was gathering a lot of information and then – the light bulb really stayed on when I was called back by a company President (some three years after I worked with him and his Admin) to work with the company's vice presidents and their executive assistants as a group.

"The President told me he and his *Admin* are 25% more efficient from what I taught them."

Twenty-five percent!

This isn't an accident.

Joan neatly ties-up these Post Graduate Level Revelations and offers them to you to use as you will – you have only to turn the page to get started.

The above was written by Marilyn Pincus. Ms. Pincus put into words *truths* that are difficult for the author to express without appearing self-serving. Joan and Marilyn have enjoyed a pleasant working relationship for many years. It's natural for each woman to serve as a "booster" for the other. Marilyn Pincus is an author and the President of Marilyn Pincus, Inc., Tucson, Arizona.

THE STAR ACHIEVEMENT®

The Star Achievement philosophy officially came to life in 1990 when I started Office Dynamics. It is alive more than ever today and has a proven track record. Star Achievement works! I can apply it to any situation and come out ahead. STAR has literally been my guiding light and the light for thousands of people who have embraced it. So what is it?

FIRST AND FOREMOST, STAR IS A PHILOSOPHY, WHICH SAYS ...

You have the potential to be a Star at work. It just takes the right combination of:

★ **Skill:** learning and enhancing business skills
★ **Attitude:** achieving and maintaining a positive attitude about your employer, your co-workers, your customers, and yourself
★ **Team:** being part of and contributing to various team relationships inside and outside the organization
★ **Strategy:** setting goals and cultivating networks to actualize your professional self

It's this four-part combination that gives you power! In other words, a person can have the skill to do the job, display a great attitude, be a team player but not know how to set goals. That person will not reach her highest level of Star performance. Or a person may know how to set goals, build team relationships, maintain a positive attitude, but not excel with the latest technology. That person will not reach the highest level she can reach in her career. When a person understands and embraces this concept, the person will continually work on developing these four key areas.

It's a way of thinking, being and performing!

Star Achievement is one of the highlights of my tenure at Rockwell Collins. Hardly a day goes by that I don't employ one of the Star doctrines – if not at work, then at home! (Pauline)

Thousands of administrative professionals have been on a Star Achievement journey since 1990 by attending Office Dynamics on-site classes. I regularly receive hand-written notes, cards, and e-mails from attendees telling me how their lives have changed. They write about:

- achieving personal goals and overcoming obstacles
- experiencing better working relationships
- advancing in their careers
- receiving awards or salary increases
- feeling more confident
- being more proactive and taking control
- organizing their work space and managing their time better
- knowing how to negotiate or persuade their manager

Even their managers and executives have written to me about the changes they have observed in their administrative professionals, such as:

- enhanced teamwork and collaboration
- more consistently positive demeanor at work
- bringing their "A-game" to work
- enables relationship development and networking with peers
- shows outstanding professionalism in difficult situations
- enhanced problem-solving techniques
- development of situational leadership skills
- understands how to excel within the corporate culture

IT IS A JOURNEY!

Wow, I've been promoted to management! If you had told me that a couple years ago, I would have laughed. Sitting there in my nice office, content with the daily routine of repetitive administrative tasks, I was more than happy to sit back and take it easy. Handling those simple jobs was a breeze and I had no desire to break a sweat much less set goals for climbing the corporate ladder. Then came Star Achievement. (Mary)

I refer to Star Achievement as a journey. If you think about going on a long trip to somewhere you have never been, what can happen to you on that trip? You probably aren't sure where to go, which areas are safe; and the people or language in that environment are unfamiliar to you. You don't feel secure. But journeys can also be fun and exciting. Sometimes you must struggle with obstacles. Flights are cancelled, luggage gets lost, a minor medical emergency occurs, or it rains eight of ten days when you are on a beach trip. You learn that you can *weather the storm*.

As you bring these principles into your life and consciously work at leveraging your talents, you may recognize it takes courage to try something new or to step out of your comfort zone. Over time, you will acquire more know-how and your inner light will shine.

STAR ACHIEVEMENT IS NOT...

Perfection! It is about being the best we can be on any given day. It involves *striving* to do a good job, producing quality work, maintaining a good attitude as you move through your day and attend to your work. It's not about being perfect, always making the right decisions, never feeling upset, or always being at the top of your game. Some days things *don't click*. It's okay as long as you realize it's okay and continue to move forward.

WHY BE A STAR ACHIEVER?

★ Work paradigms shift – you must be flexible to *keep up*
★ Rapid speed of change can surprise you/me

I know I was becoming complacent in how I did things and I felt I was extremely good at what I do. Your workshop* makes me realize I am not as good as I think I am – that is positive – (it) gives me something to strive for and will help me long term! (Kathleen)

★ Job security lies within you
★ Experience great career satisfaction and opportunities will be presented to you
★ Pure joy of knowing you are doing your best

★ It's a Way of Life ... you use it to enrich *your* life at home or away

* Joan Burge's World Class Assistant™ Certificate program.

STAR PERFORMANCE SAVES THE DAY!

In 1999, I was hosting our Annual Conference for Administrative Professionals in Virginia Beach, Virginia. One hundred and twenty five women from all over the country had arrived to participate in this event. Little did we know Hurricane Floyd was going to make an appearance too!

The powers-that-be in the City of Virginia Beach had worked with us to plan this event. Their administrative assistants were very involved in all the preparations. It was an opportunity for officials to show off their beautiful city.

As the hurricane threat escalated, the Mayor and the City's assistants were in constant contact with us. Although hotel windows that faced the ocean were covered with boards and other safety measures were implemented, we were told we would be better off to bunker down right where we were. I was told the authorities would move us if necessary and we should remain in alert-mode; ready to go, but hoping to stay.

I was responsible for 125 women and I was frightened. A few women from California left as fast as they could but what amazes me is the majority of women weren't frightened. They had great ATTITUDES. "We can get through this!" We worked as a TEAM.

We developed a STRATEGY. "If the hurricane hits during the night, and we lose power, what shall we use for light?" Fortunately that year SC Johnson was a sponsoring company. They had provided candles to use as giveaway gifts and so, we had plenty of candles to distribute. Another client had sent umbrellas. How fortuitous!

"This is where we're going to meet and this is what we're going to do." We were the only group of people left at the hotel. The hotel staff stayed with us. At 8:00 AM we formally started our event. At 10:00 AM the hurricane came through and we lost all power. We went through the entire program without electricity until power was finally restored late in the day.

Curiously, the morning of our kick-off event our scheduled speaker was Her Honor, the Mayor of Virginia Beach. I'll never forget her. She is about 5 feet tall and she is a dynamo! She had just been standing outside in the wind and rain giving an interview to reporters with CNN News about the anticipated arrival of the hurricane. She had to step on a stool at the podium so she could be seen and she stood there in her dripping wet rain parka. "If we have to get you out of here we'll do it. But, it's not going to happen!" The collective impression was … this is one confident woman. She is smart and capable and we believe in her!

Some of the attendees later told me it was the absolute best conference they ever attended! When the sun came out the next day, tee-shirts appeared with the message … *I Survived Hurricane Floyd.*

Looking back on the event, it was clear that as a group we had utilized the Star Achievement components: Skill, Attitude, Team and Strategy to help get us through and we came through brimming with pleasure and very proud of ourselves!

OVER AND OVER AGAIN

I received a letter some time ago from a student who told me she and her husband applied Star skills when they were faced with a medical emergency. They relied upon clear communication when they spoke with the doctors and medical care providers. They had to maintain positive attitudes, they looked upon all they had "to do" as a strategy for getting him better. How would they function when he returned home from the hospital? How would they handle all the pills he had to take daily?

I get so many letters praising Star Achievement methods. This happens most often when people are confronted by challenges that can overwhelm them. They rely upon Star Achievement principles to give them strength and help them move on.

Achieving Stardom

- Remember, it's a mind set.
- Focus on the 4 critical areas (skill, attitude, teamwork, strategy)
    1. look for opportunities to develop skills and attitudes in each area
    2. learn new twists to the old ways of doing things
    3. embrace brand new attitudes
    4. eliminate unproductive habits
    5. question the way things are done
- Want it! Desire is a key element to achieving Stardom.

Stepping Out of the Safety Zone is Stressful

"We have to choose between two risks. First, we can gamble on our old habits and watch our career skills gradually grow obsolete. Or we can accept the risks of the pioneer. The inventor. The explorer. The greater safety lies in choosing this second risk, even though it feels chancier than the first." —Price Pritchett

BE A POSSIBILITY THINKER

Star performers think differently. They know there is a direct relationship between their thinking and their actions. For example, if they only think about why an idea won't work, then the idea won't work. If they think about how to make the idea work, they focus on strategies and resources to make that a reality.

ACTION STEPS:

- Be positive even when things are not going quite to plan.
- Stay positive when interacting with a difficult person. Keep a good attitude and think of ways to effectively communicate with this person to diffuse anger.
- Look for the opportunity in a situation, assignment, or problem. Instead of seeing boundaries and restrictions, focus on the possibilities. This will challenge you to think creatively, use your talents, and use resources you have not used in the past.
- Remember, your thoughts drive your actions.

JOAN'S TOP TEN:

1. Be the absolute best you can be.
2. Be the president of your career.
3. Never turn in work that is "good enough." Only turn in your best.
4. Surround yourself with positive people and reading materials.
5. Allow yourself time every day for quiet and introspection.
6. Approach your manager with suggestions and solutions.
7. Motivate yourself to do things you don't like.
8. Don't give up! View barriers as opportunities.

9. Expand out if not up. It's okay to stay where you are as long as you continue to grow.
10. REACH FOR THE STARS!

UNDERNEATH IT ALL

Star Philosophy was born years before I wrote the book you're now holding in your hands. Today, I'm going to tell you what is UNDERNEATH IT ALL:

It has to do with EVOLUTION.

If you understand that as good as you are today, there are volumes and miles to go, and if you adapt the attitude that while you're on this journey you CAN evolve in positive ways –

You've Got It Made!

My father is 83 and he is still working and challenging himself. He wants to be better at golf. He schedules more time for rest but maintains a schedule that makes him feel energized and motivated and that's why my dad hasn't fully retired.

People who embrace and "live" the Star Achievement philosophy will get better and better! We don't change over night. Most of us learn through repetition. We see something over and over and sometimes we're exposed to it in different ways. I've read eight, nine, ten books from favorite business authors and even though I've heard something before … one author "says" it differently one time and suddenly it "sinks in."

Our Star Assistant is on a journey that never ends.

As you evolve you get better. You do -- if you're Star Assistant material. And, you have the added pleasure of knowing that the *best is yet to come.*

ONE

THIS IS COGNITIVE-BEING TERRITORY

Administrative Assistants who attain the *Post Graduate Level* in their profession ... are Cognitive Beings.

Worthy of mention: An Administrative Assistant need not earn a bona fide college degree. *Post Graduate* status, for our purposes, entails learning and know-how that isn't exclusive to a classroom. Moreover, Admins who earn college degrees don't automatically achieve Post Graduate status.

Q: How shall I recognize a Cognitive-Being?
A: She is someone who is fast on her feet! She follows orders and handles ordinary tasks with the best of them but, she rarely stops there. She thinks about the big-picture. She reasons ... asks why. She takes the

initiative. She is an information-gatherer and makes excellent use of her noggin!

Or, as Andy Rooney advises …

"Don't rule out working with your hands. It does not preclude using your head."

Rooney is an American journalist, correspondent, writer and producer.

How shall you recognize her?

It's likely she is looking back at you when you look into a mirror!

- A Cognitive Assistant adds value to the company.

    She doesn't confuse activity with results. Some administrative assistants work very hard but they don't get anywhere. They obtain information all day long. They must know what is important and determine what to do with that information.

    A "thinking" assistant will streamline processes; negotiate with vendors to obtain better terms, increase productivity. And, that's just for starters! For example, when a Cognitive Assistant finds herself drafting a letter for the executive she supports and editing it at least ten times; she stops! *That's too much.* She decides that five *edits* are enough. Of course, it's that same "in depth thinking" that leads her to perform a sixth edit from time to time.

    This book is loaded with illustrations of the Cognitive Being at work!
- A Cognitive Assistant doesn't settle for "top of the mind" thinking.

    In a recent Office Dynamics training workshop, there were five teams working on assignments. Team members knew they had twelve minutes to complete each segment. One team repeatedly finished ahead of the others.

You might say -- these administrative assistants are sharp! If you guessed their speed was a result of their keen abilities ... you would be mistaken. The other groups really massaged their assignments while this ahead-of-the-pack-group used "top of the mind" thinking to find their answers. They stayed in the shallow end ... didn't dig deep. In short, they probably could have done better if they remained *engaged* in the matters at hand. Instead of remaining focused on assignments they spent time chatting amicably.

This isn't to say that you can't have bright ideas quickly but Henry David Thoreau expressed it well when he said,

"Whatever sentence will bear to be read twice, we may be sure was thought twice."

Thoreau was an American essayist, poet and philosopher. 1817 – 1862.

COMMIT TO QUALITY PERFORMANCE

Did everyone in your household have a cell phone when you were a youngster? Not likely. Many young people today, however, answer this question in the affirmative. Things change.

In the 1950's some key *thinkers* recognized that if a company is to remain successful, management must take specific steps to embrace change. These pioneers developed strategies to accomplish the goal and put the philosophy of *continual improvement* on the map! New words that helped tell-the-tale popped into the business vocabulary. Kaizen, a Japanese word, which refers to "change for the better" was mentioned wherever executives gathered to learn about *continual improvement* and how-to implement it. Book store shelves sagged under the weight of the many books that appeared to expound on the topic.

You may be familiar with the name Dr. W. Edwards Deming. Dr. Deming's name is virtually synonymous with *continual improvement* and quality performance in the workplace. You may want to read more about W. Edwards Deming.

CONTINUAL IMPROVEMENT IS PART OF YOUR INHERITANCE

In Chapter Three, "I'm My Own Career-Manager and I'm "Heady" With Power!" you'll read why it's essential to maintain your competitive advantage and how *continual improvement* makes it possible. Once upon a time, people stayed with the same company for 25 years and more. The word, downsize, wasn't part of their vocabulary. That's not true any more. Companies merge, are "bought-out" and some move overseas. The Cognitive Assistant recognizes that *continual improvement* is virtually her meal-ticket! She will be retained or hired elsewhere because she is truly an asset. Her dedication to *continual improvement* enables her to thrive.

ACTION STEPS

- THINK! Remember you're a Cognitive Being.
- Add to your Daily To-Do List: practice *continual improvement*.
- Don't be in such a hurry to get a job done that you take short-cuts that sabotage results.
- Be in the moment. This means to be fully focused on what you are doing.
- Demonstrate excellence. Help raise the bar for those around you.

"If your actions inspire others to dream more, learn more, do more and become more, you are a leader."

Today's executives have much higher expectations of assistants than in the past. Many executives want assistants to learn, understand, and especially "know" the business. If you absolutely can't wait to read more about this; turn to Chapter Six; "The Anatomy of A Strategic Partnership." Of course, you'll also read about this in Chapter Four; "Professionalism Works For Me." Many of the topics discussed in *Underneath It All* spill over from one chapter into another. Since it takes a Cognitive Being to earn a place on the executive team ... you'll also read more about this phenomenon when you read chapter Five; "Earning Your Rightful Place On The Executive Team." And, so it goes.

SELF-MANAGEMENT

Our thoughts CAN get us into trouble. For example, a negative thought about a particular situation causes you to feel upset. If you "manage" or, change your thought, you will probably change your response. Instead of feeling hurt, you may focus on being empathetic and get to the source of the problem.

Susan's tardiness is completely out-of-character. She makes me look bad because I can't complete the report without those figures. I'm going to blow the deadline.

I wonder if she still has troubles at home. That's no excuse for poor performance at work but it can happen. I will call her into my office right after lunch and ask her to explain.

NOW OR NEVER

Many people react to an event or, to other peoples' actions based upon how they feel at that moment. Sometimes that's good. Sometimes, it's not. When you become good at self-management, you won't give in to knee-jerk reactions. You'll pause and think before you act. When you pause to "manage" your thoughts and assess conclusions, you may decide to do nothing at all. This can be especially effective when you have negative thoughts about a person or event. Self-management, under these circumstances, helps to define you as the consummate professional.

ACTION STEPS

- Take responsibility for your "intellect" – don't jump to conclusions.
- Be ready to banish negative thinking or negative reactions. Stop. Regroup. And choose to handle the situation calmly and tactfully.
- Compose yourself. Maintain unshakable poise when challenged by events or people.
- Continue to learn. Pay particular attention to your job, your company and industry but don't stop there. Devour general information too. Consider it a compliment if someone calls you a news-junkie! Your out-put is heavily dependent on in-put!

SELF-MOTIVATION – THAT LEADS US TO ENGAGEMENT

If you feel bored, stagnant, or overwhelmed, maybe you are not putting enough positive energy into your work. Decide to look for the good in your job and how to make it more fun.

Motivation Is An Inside Job!

Believe – in yourself; in your ability to learn and to make wise decisions. No one knows you better than you. We have to keep our belief a solid foundation so that when others doubt us, we can stay strong.

Responsible – realizing we have to motivate ourselves. We still need others to support us and then we take responsibility for our actions and the outcomes.

Inspire yourself – by reading positive materials; using positive self-talk; and being optimistic.

Commit yourself – to showing up mentally every day; to a cause; to something that inspires and motivates you.

Know yourself – play to your strengths; build rapport with those who support your weaknesses and continue to develop your weak areas.

Surround yourself – with people who are energetic, enthusiastic and are cheerleaders!

<u>BRICKS – build your positive attitude with a strong base of self motivation.</u>

> *"We limit ourselves by the way we think. Star Assistants think differently! They are possibility thinkers."*
> —Joan Burge

EMPLOYEE ENGAGEMENT

"A recent Gallup Employee Engagement Index Poll found that only 29% of workers are truly "engaged," that is, they work with passion and feel a profound connection to their company. Another survey found that at least 20% of employees are either actively or passively job hunting."

(Source: reported on the Web:
http://www.prweb.com/releases/2007/3/prweb514625.htm)

This source refers to: Workforce Engagement: Strategies to Attract, Motivate and Retain Talent by Stephen Hundley, PH.D., Frederic Jacobs, Ph.D. and Marc Drizin. The authors repeatedly refer to studies conducted by the Performance Assessment Network (PAN) in 2004-2005 and 2006-2007. So, the figures are timely.

The more engaged you are in the office – the more you *genuinely* care about some aspect of your work and when you do; your career contributes to a rewarding personal life. Almost without exception, highly successful people are "present" in a way many others are not. They participate actively in their lives, rather than sit on the sidelines. Take a few moments to ask yourself these four questions to find out how engaged you are right now, at this very moment:

ACTIVITY:

1. **What's the one thing I want and need to accomplish today** to feel I've made progress toward my personal dreams and goals in life?
   - <u>Hint</u>: This can be a small thing with big ramifications just ahead. For example, "I need to set aside an hour today to review my calendar so I'm even more organized, confident, efficient and productive in the month ahead."

_____

_____

_____

2. **How committed am I?** For instance, if it means working a little longer, or bringing the task home (even to think about it), am I willing to invest in my future without viewing it as a "sacrifice"? Am I willing to *go the distance*?

    - <u>Hint</u>: If, as Woody Allen said, 80% of success is just showing up, what can you do to get closer to 100%?

    _____

    _____

    _____

    _____

3. **Who do I want to acknowledge** for his or her assistance in helping me achieve a recent success?

    - <u>Hint</u>: The more you value and appreciate the positive impact others have on your life, the more connected they are to you – and the more engaged you become.

    _____

    _____

    _____

    _____

One of my clients tells me he has a "dream" assistant named Deborah. It's as though Deborah "dreams" the future/his future and takes steps to make things easier/better/more successful for him. He had to be in China for the entire month prior to his industry's annual gathering. He was a popular presenter who attracted large audiences when he spoke at these gatherings. In addition to working diligently to prepare his presentations, he worked to fill the auditorium. "We maintain a list of the 2008 attendees and a list of those who are registered to hear me speak during the 2009 gathering. Deborah knows I compare the lists and call those 2008 attendees who haven't yet registered to be with us in 2009. People generally appreciate this personal call and respond favorably. This time, instead of turning over two lists to me ... Deborah gave me one list. *Can you think why?* She gave me the 2008 list with some names *highlighted* in blue. These are the names of people I need to call. My previous assistant never thought of this nor did I. But, Deborah is a Cognitive Being. Her strategy probably decreased the time I normally spend on the task by 60%." *Deborah, if it weren't for your innovative approach to this task, I'd spend considerable extra time contacting people. I appreciate your creativity and I thank you.*

You may want to acknowledge the supplier who worked on the weekend just so he could deliver the merchandise on Monday. This, after you discovered, the purchase order was never sent to him. You may want to acknowledge the Human Resource Director for introducing you to employees who carpool to work. You traveled with them the weeks your vehicle was in the body shop. How about the vendor at the lobby newsstand? He reserved copies of magazines for you when your company was featured on the front page. You actually learned about the article from him.

4. **Who or what do I need to address** about an issue that's hampering my effectiveness, and therefore, my success?

     - <u>Hint</u>: Engaged people want to tackle problems, processes and issues that can be improved upon for everyone's benefit. They address them professionally and objectively, like a person solving a puzzle – not a bewildered soul lost in a maze! Instead, like Einstein or Edison, they have endless faith and a vision for what can be. As you consider the answer to this question, don't be surprised if you reach back into the past. There may be an issue

that nags at you from time to time but continues to be
unresolved.

_____

_____

_____

_____

It Happened To Me

I didn't have to look far to find a story that illustrates the tremendous
worth of a Cognitive Being.

Jasmine Freeman is my Chief Executive Assistant and she is TOPS! She
tells me she didn't have to think too hard about saying YES to the job offer
but from the instant she entered "my world" she had to think and think and
think again!

She came to work at Office Dynamics when my equilibrium had been
torpedoed on several fronts. A routine physical exam resulted in an
unexpected diagnosis. I had to have abdominal surgery and had to move
quickly. I was scheduled to leave for California in two days to host my
annual conference for 125 women and I was the main speaker. I had never
had major surgery and I was petrified. I got the necessary blood work done
so I could be admitted to the hospital as soon as I returned from California.
While I was in California, my younger sister called me to tell me our dad was
very sick and hospitalized in Cleveland. I'm close with my dad and I was
heartsick. I couldn't immediately get on a plane and fly to be with him and
as we spoke on the phone, he was in tears because of his pain. He's a tough
guy so, this was just killing me. At almost the same time, we got word that
my mother-in-law was rushed to a hospital in Texas. I made it through the
conference without anyone knowing my "mental state" and made it through
the surgery. But, after surgery, there were some complications and I was in

no condition to fly. Every day we were on the telephone; how is my dad? How is my mother-in-law? How am I??? In the meantime, Jasmine and I had been conducting long-distance interviews and I offered her the job. I thought to myself, why would she want to come, she must think I'm insane! (I'll share more of the story with you in later chapters but this much information helps you to understand some of what Jasmine faced right from the get-go.) I wasn't able to train Jasmine and since no one else worked at this office who knew the ins and outs like me, no one was there to offer assistance; answer questions. Jasmine was in a city that was completely new to her, in an office that was very different from her former work environment. She had left her husband and children behind in Iowa. They were to follow in three weeks. I was so excited that she was here but I got progressively worse before I got better. Jasmine was so patient with me. There were days when I had such bad anxiety I had to ask her to sit with me while I ate lunch. I knew I had to pull myself together to save my business but I also knew I didn't want to lose Jasmine and this fact helped motivate me. There were days I didn't come to the office but I was able to give Jasmine the basics regarding how to handle phone calls. We broke everything down to basics. Jasmine reflects, "I had to get my arms around the basics. That's all we had time to deal with but I think they were what kept the business going in the early weeks when Joan was out."

Jasmine had some office procedures booklets to read but essentially she had to rely upon herself. She had to get up-to-speed quickly on what this business entailed and what was important to clients. She took initiative; located and contacted a former assistant who was helpful. Day by day, she kept things afloat. I think of Jasmine as a woman of courage, conviction, dedication and more. I know, without a doubt, that she is a Cognitive Being!

Robots need not apply. Many people mindlessly tackle tasks and obtain adequate results. The Cognitive Being, however, is (with rare exception) fully engaged from the time she walks in the door until closing time.

Q: How do I stay fully engaged day-in and day-out?
A: Look forward to coming to work! It's easy when you're a *Player.*

It's not up to management to keep you *fully engaged.* It's up to you to do what is necessary to make your work challenging and fulfilling. Authors Jackie and Kevin Freiberg wrote, *BOOM!: 7 Choices for Blowing the Doors Off Business As Usual.*

Chapter #1 is entitled, "Be a Player." Chapter #7 is entitled "Risk More – Gain More." Can you see where this leads? *No way* will you do things by rote when you're *fully engaged!* Admittedly, during the early months of Dave's cancer diagnosis and treatment, I was overwhelmed. Even when I tried to manage my thoughts I came up "empty." But, this was an extreme situation and I finally had to tell myself that things would simply wait. Underneath It All it's rare, if ever, that you will face extreme challenges. Most of your work life you can be fully engaged and reap the fantastic benefits that come with the territory.

Two

I've Got What it Takes to be a Leader

"Good leadership consists of showing average people how to do the work of superior people."
—John D. Rockefeller, American industrialist and philanthropist. 1839-1937

The following **Underneath It All** observations put leadership under a microscope. As you read each segment ask yourself; *how am I doing?*

BE A PROFESSIONAL AGENT FOR YOUR COMPANY

You are an ambassador or agent for your company. You interact and communicate with internal and external customers, community leaders and vendors. You represent not only yourself; you represent the people you support. You sometimes act as an agent on their behalf, sharing information and giving directions. You are an extension of your executive. When you are a true professional, you gain the respect of those with whom you interact. You're taken seriously and inspire others.

Scoring: Give yourself a numerical rating of 1, 2, 3, 4 or 5 as you answer – *How am I doing* as a company agent/ambassador? 1 = TOPS. 5 = NEEDS IMPROVEMENT.

HAVING THE COURAGE TO BE THE BEST

It takes courage and stamina to wake each morning and say, "I will make the most of every minute!" Here are some ways to bolster your courage to live more fully and enjoy greater success in all your endeavors. Remember, as you become the best you can be; people around you will be encouraged to be their best. (Mr. Rockefeller (see above) would, no doubt, agree!)

Scoring: Give yourself a numerical rating of 1, 2, 3, 4 or 5 as you answer – I know I have courage and stamina but do others know it too? *How am I doing?* 1 = TOPS. 5 = NEEDS IMPROVEMENT.

LIVE HONESTLY

I'm not talking here about following rules and regulations and being a good person. That's a given. I mean this: Strive at all times to be true to your authentic self. If you live what you believe – and consciously use your words and deeds to reflect those beliefs (not always easy, mind you) – you'll *own* your life and the way you live it. You'll be the best you can be and experience great satisfaction in all you do.

Scoring: Give yourself a numerical rating of 1, 2, 3, 4 or 5 as you answer – *Does the real me come shining through most of the time?* 1 = TOPS. 5 = NEEDS IMPROVEMENT.

EMBRACE CHANGE

Change is the only constant in life, so why ignore it; sidestep or, fight it? Instead, view it as an opportunity! Choose to become a part of the action, rather than the human equivalent of flotsam or jetsam, tossed hither and yon without exerting any will.

Scoring: Give yourself a numerical rating of 1, 2, 3, 4 or 5 as you answer – *Do I willingly embrace change?* 1 = TOPS. 5 = NEEDS IMPROVEMENT.

KEEP AN OPEN MIND

Human beings *cannot* know everything, no matter how hard they try. We must be endlessly inquisitive and change our minds when necessary. No one said it's easy but the benefits far outweigh the negatives – namely, apathy and stagnation.

Scoring: Give yourself a numerical rating of 1, 2, 3, 4 or 5 as you answer – *Do I approach new information with an open mind?* 1 = TOPS. 5 = NEEDS IMPROVEMENT.

BE ADVENTUROUS

Today is a new day, no matter how similar it may seem to yesterday, tomorrow, next week or month. Sculpt today as you would sculpt a piece of clay. *What would make this day outstanding?* Be willing to step out of your comfort zone and make a difference.

Scoring: Give yourself a numerical rating of 1, 2, 3, 4 or 5 as you answer – *Am I sufficiently adventurous?* 1 = TOPS. 5 = NEEDS IMPROVEMENT.

JOTTINGS!

Consider other ways you can display personal courage to be your best and find adventure in everything you do. That's what makes a true "star" at work and home. Let that commitment to live an excellent life shine through, starting today! Clearly, you've got what it takes to be a LEADER!

_____

_____

_____

_____

FACING FEAR

There are times when F-E-A-R is nothing more than -- False Evidence Appearing Real.

We all have experienced it. Fear comes in different sizes and shapes, has different faces, and the things I fear, you might find quizzical and vice versa.

The big difference between people is that for some, fear paralyzes and for others fear becomes a personal challenge. It gets their adrenalin pumping. Every time you confront your fears, you become a stronger person. You prepare yourself for bigger and greater things to come. This isn't to say that once you conquer a fear you will never again be afraid. It's just that when you learn to deal with a fear and experience some success in taking it on, you will be more inclined to take on the next worrisome challenge and come out on top!

A LEADER IDENTIFIES & UTILIZES SURVIVAL TACTICS

Fear can prevent an individual from going where she wants to go on the career path. Underneath It All there's no good reason to succumb to this consequence. Muster your courage and ....

1. **Get more information.** It's a waste of time and energy to be fearful based upon hearsay or sketchy information. American businessman, Franklin P. Jones (1887 – 1929) is quoted as follows: "I find that a great part of the information I have was acquired by looking up something and finding something else on the way."

2. **Refuse to dwell on your fear.** Be aware that fear can become a monster. If you give it room to grow; it becomes bigger in your mind than it really is. Ask yourself if you're likely to remember this fear six months from now. Put the fear into perspective and it's likely to lose some wallop!

3. **Remember the thought of doing something that scares you is likely to be more difficult to handle than the actual experience.** (Think of it as the making a mountain out of a molehill syndrome!) This is especially true if you're a creative individual with a good imagination. This is one time you don't want to give your imagination free reign.

4. **Think through the fear and ask – what is it that really makes me afraid?** Am I afraid of failure? Am I afraid of disappointing others? Then, ask – can I do something in advance to ameliorate the consequences. For example, you may speak with ease to small gatherings but when numbers increase and you must use a microphone you choke-up. Ask for the groups to be divided and

make two presentations or, check with audio experts. Another kind of voice amplification system may be more to your liking.

5. **Think f-a-r ahead.** Anticipate the worst possible outcome if you do what you fear; decide what you will do should that occur and whether you can live with that situation. If you can't live with the outcome, or don't want to, perhaps you should decline to participate. We're not all good at everything and that's all there is to it. But, don't slink off without making plans to satisfy needs. Can a surrogate handle this challenge for you?

6. **Accentuate the positive.** Look for all the good things that could happen if you take on the challenge. Now is the time to let your imagination reign free.

7. **Develop a Contingency Plan.** This plan is especially practical when there are many outside factors you don't control. Extreme weather conditions, flight delays, cancellations can wreak havoc on some business events … if you're the go-to-person; what then? If you have some idea of how to deal with obstacles, you'll boost your confidence level and take the sting out of your fears.

8. **Take a deep breath and go for it!**
    a. Some ways to display courage at work are: deal with a colleague who is ignoring the negative consequences of his or her actions, present a new idea to management, be honest with a coworker or learn new things.
    b. Know that it is okay to feel fearful but display courage by taking action. Mark Twain wrote, "Courage is resistance to fear; mastery of fear—not absence of fear."

c. Develop a diplomatically *assertive* attitude. Aggressive people only care about themselves and their needs. Passive people only care about others and what they think. *Assertive* people care about their own needs and getting the job done *while* caring about others.

d. Stand out from the crowd in terms of doing the right thing. For example, just because everyone else in your department takes extra break time, doesn't mean you should.

e. Ask for something "unusual." You want to boost your skills by attending one or two business workshops. This is unheard of at your company. You step into your executive's office armed with details; ask for time off to attend and for reimbursement of the registration fee.

Take Charge

Having an "attitude of taking charge" is not necessarily the same as the "skill of taking charge." It starts with having the attitude, then developing certain skills. When you recognize this *truth* and fully subscribe to it, you will see your work differently. Instead of waiting around for others to tell you what to do or assign the next task, you will anticipate what needs to be done and do it. Occasionally, you will take a risk and act on an idea before being asked to do so. You will be seen as a leader and will be given more challenging assignments.

> *"It is our attitude at the beginning of a difficult*
> *undertaking which, more than anything else, will*
> *determine its successful outcome."*
> —William James, American philosopher and psychologist, 1842 – 1910

ACTION STEPS

- When you *see* a problem, determine whether you have the ability and resources to work on it or can it be better managed by a co-worker, manager, or people in another department.
- Take charge of your viewpoint. Just because a co-worker is negative about a change at work, doesn't mean you have to agree with that individual.
- See the proverbial *next step* and take action. Instead of waiting for your manager to tell you the next step, see if you can determine what that next step will be.

LEADERS CHOOSE THEIR ATTITUDES

You don't control other people and circumstances.

You do control yourself. This is a powerful truth!

People's attitudes tend to spiral up or down depending on what is going on or how they feel. A person needs to realize he or she decides how to respond to any set of circumstances. (By the way, this ties back to self-management which was mentioned earlier.)

MAKE THE RIGHT CHOICE

Every time you are challenged by an individual, thrown into a difficult situation or faced with a hectic day, you have a choice:

- be happy and continue on with your day
- be upset and let your entire day be ruined

Life will always toss challenges at you. There will often be a "Nancy Negative" or, "Don Dragon" who upsets you. You can make the decision every morning that you will face whatever comes your way with poise and tact.

If you make this a daily practice, before you know it, you won't have to think about what to do, or make a concentrated effort to do it. It will come naturally, and you will find yourself a happier, more peaceful and more productive person.

> You cannot tailor-make the situations in life, but you can tailor-make the attitudes to fit those situations.

Rejuvenating Your Attitude

<u>Renewal should be a daily process</u>. We are surrounded by and exposed to a great deal of bad news. It is important to fill your mind with positive readings and thoughts every day. Think about it: you feed your body with food to stay healthy; you may take vitamins to provide additional nutrients. You have to *feed your* mind positive thoughts every day.

<u>An occasional major renewal may be needed</u>. Every once in a while life throws you too many curves and it's a bit much to handle many changes at once. You many need to take a 3-day retreat and get away from it all. When you realize that synonyms for "renew" are: rejuvenate, reinstate, mend, repair, restore – it's immediately clear that "renewal" brings out some of the best you have to offer.

<u>Have a sense of humor; laugh</u>. I remember when I was a little girl, my dad used to say, "Joan Marie – you are so serious. Smile!" I tend to be on the more serious side. I'm not like my older sister, Janet, who makes us laugh all the time. In our family, we call her our "Lucille Ball." She has a great sense of humor. Well, as I said, I tend to take life and work more seriously. So I know I have to learn to lighten up once in a while.

<u>Focus on the wins in your life and reward yourself</u>. Every week we have "wins," large or small. We tend to focus on what we didn't accomplish. I've

heard this is especially true of women. Instead think about the many things you accomplish in a day.

<u>Act, don't react</u>.   This is especially true when we are dealing with someone at work with whom we are upset. We tend to use our emotions. Use your brain and think about how to respond in a way that will get the results you want.

<u>Use positive self-talk</u>.   Do you know we talk to ourselves all day long? We're either saying something positive or negative. Say things like, "I can do this." "I will get this done today." "I can manage that difficult person with professionalism."

<u>Focus on self-change vs. changing others</u>.   This is especially true when you have to work with someone who is not going to change his or her ways or attitude. You have a choice. You can continue to focus on what you don't like about this individual or look for the one or two good contributions the person makes.

<u>Be aware of negative messages sent by coworkers and friends</u>.   Really listen. They may cause you to take actions you normally would not take. Surround yourself with positive people.

Remember that when you can't control the situation, you can choose your attitude about the situation.

Choose to preserve your good attitude.
Ignore or avoid chronically negative people.
Remember that it's OK to level with negative people.
Believe in yourself.
Commit to goals. They are important to
self-satisfaction, confidence, and professional growth.
Keep your attitude in shape by reading motivational
books and listening to CDs in the car.

> *Be aware of negative messages being sent by*
> *co-workers or friends.*
> *Tune out other people's doubts and fears.*

EFFECTS OF ATTITUDE ON HEALTH & LONGEVITY

- Stress can ravage the body, unless the mind says no. A positive outlook can reduce the impact of stress on health. *(USA Today)*
- Take this to heart: Happy people live longer than dour fuddy-duddies. *(USA Today)*
- Attitude makes all the difference. *(Mind, Body & Soul by ppplv.com)*
- Nun's story of aging… study links sharp minds to a positive mindset. *(USA Today)*
- The secrets to longevity. *(USA Today)*
- Optimists keep smiling. A study published by Mayo Clinic found that people who have optimistic outlooks live longer and healthier lives than their pessimistic counterparts. *(mayohealth.org)*
- The power of positive thinking. Decades of research by Gallup has suggested that increasing positive emotions can expand a person's lifespan by as much as 10 years. *(Real Simple)*

POWER UP YOUR ATTITUDE!™

BUILD SELF-CONFIDENCE AND A POSITIVE MENTAL IMAGE.

- Make the change in your thinking from "problem" to "opportunity."

For example, it would be easy to feel frustrated if you've just spent the last two days showing executives from another country some of the outstanding city sites only to learn they already took this tour. *Were they too polite to tell you so?* Instead of saying, "This reflects poorly on me, my partner and our company," put another "face" on the situation. "Our business guests should feel very important because two completely different company leaders gave them this prized tour." In the future, however, ask where foreign visitors have been and where they would like to go before making tour plans. If time permits, you may want to do this with the current group of executives.

COMBAT NEGATIVITY

- Listen to what you're saying to yourself. Instead of saying, "Nothing seems to be going right today," mentally rephrase it to, "Wow, I'm really being challenged today to think creatively." You are in control of your own thinking. You can change that old record and stop feeling like a victim. You can get support from family and friends, but you ultimately have to take responsibility for your own attitude. Your sister may tell you that you look happy in the company photograph but if you tell yourself … "happy" helps her avoid telling me that I gained weight! -- you sabotage a compliment. Don't.

- Set goals and make a specific plan for your career. When you measure progress you feel in-control. If your company offers continuing education opportunities, for example, when you complete two out of four successfully; "notify" yourself that you're half way through the program. The *proverbial glass* is half-full and not half-empty. Most importantly, this is a solid achievement – one that is easily measured so you can hardly argue the point.

CAN YOU CHANGE A PERSON'S BAD ATTITUDE?
(EXCERPT FROM JOAN BURGE'S STAR MANAGER™ SERIES)

While you may choose to surround yourself with positive thinkers, you can't always avoid working with (or sometimes, living with) negative thinkers. Therein lies a problem: What can you do to change a person's inherently bad attitude, in part so it doesn't affect you? And should you try?

Here are a few observations that can help:

- <u>People are who they are.</u> Like spouses or children, they don't "change" because you will it. So exerting your influence and expecting the response you want is foolhardy at best and potentially disastrous for your relationship at worst.

- <u>Try to empathize, even a little.</u> Remember: Life is not fair, and it can be harder on some than others. People who feel defeated or alone in the world still have to wake up each morning and eke out a living like the rest of us. We don't have to know the exact reasons behind their troubles to see the cloud that surrounds them at work, and to pause a moment and wish that weren't so – for their sakes more than ours.

- <u>Reach out as you're able.</u> Make an effort to connect and be friendly – more than once, if need be. People with poor attitudes tend to be protective and distrusting – and may not initially welcome your friendship, perhaps because they fear there are "strings" attached. Be gentle in your persistence. It'll reinforce your sincerity, likely earning their trust and a better attitude in the process.

When a person's bad attitude cannot be tempered by the above methods, yet still needs to be addressed for the benefit of the workplace, you need to consider constructively confronting the situation. Many times, informing people of their bad attitude in a positive way (i.e., "I thought you'd want to know the impact that X, Y or Z is having on the rest of the department, because I'm confident that's not how you meant to be perceived...") can help influence change.

Ask yourself, "Is their attitude a daily event or due to behind-the-scenes circumstances?"

A TRUE STORY FROM JOAN BURGE...

A few weeks before I was getting ready to teach Part 3 of my World Class Assistant™ program, one of my attendees (Ginny; not her real name) e-mailed me and asked that I not make her share a Success Story with the other attendees as was planned on the class agenda. (Because attendees have been together at past sessions, I ask them to share the successes they've experienced since the last time they met.) She said that she was going through something very personal and was afraid she would get emotional in front of the group. I didn't pry and ask what was going on. I always feel if someone wants to share something personal with me, they will. Class day arrived and everyone but Ginny shared their Success Story. Throughout the two-day program, there also were other times when Ginny chose not to speak or answer questions in front of the group.

One of my trainers who was also attending this program and was not aware of the e-mail I received prior to the event asked Ginny on the second day if she was afraid to speak in front of others. Did it make her nervous? Ginny broke down in tears and told my trainer that her husband had been diagnosed with stage 4 cancer just a few months ago.

27

This is a perfect example of how we really don't know what is going on with others. Sometimes one of your co-workers may be going through something personal that affects his or her attitude at work, and other times, there are company employees who always have a negative attitude for no discernible reasons. It is their way of life. A Star Assistant will learn how to differentiate between the two and act accordingly.

THE NUTS AND BOLTS OF LEADING

Keep cool under pressure. When you feel pressured, you tend not to think as clearly and may respond to situations and people in a way you later regret. The quality of your work may even suffer. When working under pressure, just do the best you can. Remember, you are one person with only so many hours in the day. If something doesn't get done today, you always have tomorrow. In our "do it now/overnight it yesterday/instant-message me" society, people feel like they have to get all their work done now. Slow down and work smarter.

Be known as an action person. This means do what you say you will do. This is so simple, yet most people don't follow through. You can also enhance your image by coming up with new ideas and solutions to problems and then implementing them. If you realize you can't follow through on something you agreed to accomplish, acknowledge it as soon as possible and explain why you can't. Just don't make a habit of not fulfilling your commitments, or your credibility in the workplace may suffer.

Know when to take risks. Risk-taking can be dangerous and scary, but it can also pay big dividends. Weigh your options, consider possible outcomes, and then act accordingly.

Take charge. People respond more positively when you clearly communicate your needs and establish deadlines while still respecting their needs. Taking charge also means responding to negative behavior rather than letting people get away with inappropriate actions.

Don't procrastinate. Buckle down to unpleasant or difficult tasks.

Allow yourself vision. This comes more naturally to some people than others. Think about possibilities, what could be; don't be limited by the status quo.

Exude energy. Being a leader is a great responsibility as well as an honor because good leaders impact lives. Inspire those around you with your enthusiasm and energy. You may not always feel that way inside, but if you act energetic, you often start to feel it.

Keep fears and doubts to yourself. Even leaders sometimes have fears and question their decisions. They can get frustrated with people they're coaching. Choose a close friend or peer whom you trust. That individual will listen to you *vent*. Don't get carried off, however, get back to accentuating the positive fast.

Seek mentors. Avoid the trap of believing that, due to your experience and success, "you know everything." We can always learn from others.

Believe in what you are doing. Believe in the cause – the mission. Then, when the going gets tough and you feel like quitting because that would be the easiest thing to do, you'll stick it out and reap the rewards of your efforts over time.

Build physical/mental energy. If you want to be a good leader and create a path for the future, these are necessities. There is no room for *whimps* on this journey!

Accept chaos as a pre-existing condition, and avoid struggling against it.

Be a good role model. You shouldn't tell co-workers something and ignore it yourself. An example is telling people to be on time for staff meetings and then arriving late yourself. Walk your talk!

Be consistent. Consistency in the way you treat and speak to each colleague is important. It will boost your credibility, and people with whom you work will respect you more.

Ask for input. Do you know what your strategic partner thinks or wants regarding a specific issue? Find out: Say something like, "What do you need from me so you can put all your energy into this project?"

Be a Star Assistant every day. You can't be a Star one day, then slack off the next day and expect to remain a good role model. This does not mean that you have to be perfect, or that you're not going to have "bad" days. You will. Get over it!

MENTORING

Mentoring, in its most basic form, refers to one person teaching another. Mentoring relationships often develop on an informal basis, as a result of one person working closely with another person. Any working relationship has the potential to be a mentoring situation.

> *"Successful people turn everyone who can help them into*
> *sometime mentors!"*
> —John Crosby

BE A ROLE MODEL OF SUCCESS

You are always on stage. Whether you are on the telephone, walking down the hall at work, walking into your executive's office or attending a meeting, you are on stage. People are constantly watching you and how you act. Once you have acted or spoken, you may wish you didn't but it's too late. You are in a position to positively influence others. When you act professional and emulate success, you encourage others to raise their levels of performance. Again, you increase your value to the organization and are perceived as credible and influential.

ACTION STEPS:

- A mentor is a wise and trusted counselor. You can be a mentor at any time to any person.
- Other administrative peers at other levels in the organization are watching you. They form views and opinions about the profession based on how they see those in the profession act. Be proud of your chosen profession.
- Being a Role Model of Success is an every day event. You can't be a top performer one day and be mediocre the next two days. It's also not about perfection. It's *striving* to be and do your best every day.
- Lead by example. Actions speak louder than words.

AS A MENTOR

Sharing wisdom with a fellow employee boosts your training skills. You even master the art of coaching – when you offer constructive criticism. These are admirable skills – skills you will need to succeed in the workplaces of today and tomorrow.

Set an example of professionalism: Demonstrate a strong work ethic to a mentee who is eager to follow your lead. By showing your mentee the right way to do things, you help your company create a more qualified pool of employees and show you are a team player.

Be prepared to give and take. When questions are asked, mentors must be patient. Make no judgments ... just answer the questions.

It Happened to Me

Once Upon A Time – early in my career
I experienced excellent mentoring and never forgot it.

As a new hire

- The Personnel Department Director greeted me; we shook hands and she told me I had a *Free Pass*. She smiled and explained that during this first week on the job, I was a MVP – Most Valued Person. Only new hires were entitled to a Free Pass.
- I received an attractive Kit that was labeled, Survival Kit. A Kit was issued to each newly salaried employee.
- I got a personal tour of the 12 floor building.
- I was encouraged to ask questions. My company-liaison answered without hesitation.
- My supervisor took me to lunch off premises. I don't remember the name of the restaurant but I remember linen table cloths and attractive surroundings.
- I was introduced to many people and each invited me to "stay in touch."

I was hired as an Administrative Assistant and very quickly learned the people who hired me expected me to flourish. They gave me a good send off into what was to become a ten year stint! I have sometimes wondered if I would have plunged into the work so enthusiastically if I had not been greeted so warmly.

Be Your Own Cheerleader

"Trust yourself. Create the kind of self that you will be happy to live with all your life. Make the most of yourself by fanning the tiny, inner sparks of possibility into flames of achievement."
—Gold Meir, Israeli founder and Prime Minister,
1898 - 1978

- Catch yourself doing things well.
- Use positive self-talk.
- Let people know about your talents. *You don't have to shout your praises from the rooftops but everyone will hear you if you do.*
- Do not let other people's pessimism or negative attitudes get you down. Brush it off and move on.
- Keep a "Success Journal" at work.
- At the end of each day, reflect on one thing you did well.

UNDERNEATH IT ALL

You aren't always going to do or say the right thing; make the perfect decision; react in the most professional way. The people you *look up to* don't always do or say the right thing either.

Jeannette Scollard (author of *Risk to Win*, Macmillan Publishing) writes, "Women too often shy away from risk in their lives, seeing it in terms of danger and possible failure rather than challenge and opportunity. This conditioned reflex can limit a woman's chances for advancement and fulfillment in her career."

Underneath It All … No one is perfect. Still, you can be a superb leader. You can be superwoman!

I know that what works today probably won't be sufficient to *get me through* tomorrow. My continuing education is just that … continuing! Attending lectures and workshops and reading books that are relevant to the times, my career, and my industry are part of the rhythm of my life. I discuss what I uncover with people who share my *intensity* to be excellent! In short, I invest in me. I don't wait for someone in the company to send me to a seminar. If the company were to disappear tomorrow, I would still be a leader.

Bette Midler wrote, *"My idea of superwoman is someone who scrubs her own floors."* Ms. Midler is an American singer and actress, born in 1945.

I think her observation is brilliant!!

I can do it-all if I must and … you can do the same.

THREE

I'm My Own Career-Manager and I'm "Heady" with Power!

When you think "career" as opposed to "job" you are more likely to get serious!

After all, "career" suggests a long-term involvement and promising rewards.

Go ahead, take a bow … after all you're in control and are overflowing with power. Of course, this is only true if you recognize that it's true.

A recent college graduate was looking through a magnifying glass as she helped her young niece study the petals on a flower. She was struck by the thought that she could study her current job search better if she held the process up to serious scrutiny. As soon as she positioned her thinking in this direction … she felt "heady" with power! She was usually quiet when she was being interviewed; answering only the questions she was asked. Now, she decided to ask some very specific questions of the interviewer. "After all, she mused, "I want to work for a company that will offer me opportunities to learn and grow." She reasoned that she could position herself well right from the get-go. She realized she was new to the business world but she was a capable person who could think-on-her-feet.

> *"Too many people overvalue what they are not and*
> *undervalue what they are."*
> —Malcolm S. Forbes

Take Pride in Your Profession:
Synonyms for Pride:
Choice
Dignity
Elite
Glory In
Self-esteem
Self-respect

Stand tall and feel good about what you do and the position you hold and you'll feel energized. This energy assists you to perform well and to be happy. It's a lovely cycle that perpetuates itself and it all begins with your perception.

Conduct a two question perception check:

- Are you proud of yourself?
- If not, why not?

(Observation: It could be that you're too hard on yourself and don't recognize your attributes or, it could be that you're in the wrong place so far as your job is concerned. If you're too tough on yourself – cut it out! If you're in the wrong place, set your sights on moving elsewhere and then, take steps to get there.)

Pledge to Be Proud

I pledge to be proud of the career I have chosen.

I choose to hold my head high in front of others at work.

I commit to being a positive representative for all administrative professionals.

I know I have value and add worth to my organization.

I will continue to elevate other's perceptions of this role.

I want to be a positive role model for novice administrative professionals.

I pledge to be proud to be an Administrative Professional!

CAREER ANALYSIS

- Where do you want to be in 1 year? 3 years? 5 years?
- What are you good at (e.g., cooperating with others, working alone, communicating, moving from place to place as opposed to reporting to an office day in/day out)?
- What type of industry would you enjoy working in?
- How much are you willing to invest in your future (e.g., staying late, continuing formal education or job training)?
- Do you want to move out of the profession some day?
- Do you want to look for other opportunities in your current company (whether in the administrative profession or not)?

IDENTIFY AND EVALUATE ROADBLOCKS TO ATTAINING JOB SATISFACTION

The following questions serve as a starting place:

- What are some obstacles that stand in your way to being more productive?
- What is one thing you would like your executive to: do, stop doing, or do more often? (e.g., praise my performance, offer constructive criticism, keep me better informed about things in general).
- What strengths do you bring to your role and executive?
- What areas do you think you need to develop?

> *"When you come to a roadblock, take a detour."*
> —Barbara Bush, American first lady 1989-93

NAVIGATE YOUR CAREER

Part of being professional is setting goals and navigating your career. Determining goals, stating them clearly and creating a plan are the hardest tasks for individuals. Many people don't get what they want; or achieve their career goals because it takes work! Once you determine what you want and write your plan, the road gets a little easier. But you have to learn how to implement the plan, monitor your progress, and overcome barriers. The benefits derived can be said in simple terms: *"If you don't plan where you want to go, you will go wherever life and others take you. And that may not be where you want to end up!"* When you take charge of your career, you will feel fulfilled. You will also know how to reroute yourself when things at work aren't going your way; how to get back on course when changes occur at work, such as a partner leaving the company, or the company downsizes.

And, don't forget to add retirement planning to your *map*. If you're at the beginning of your career, this may not enter your thoughts. Clearly, a plan needs tweaking as time goes by. So, tweak!

Illustration A: Meg was 27 years old and the mother of twins. She and her spouse wanted to be in an excellent position to pay for the twins' college education. This realization hit her hard when the twins celebrated their fifth birthdays. She calculated that in five years time she could double her salary. She was a college graduate but she wasn't a good writer and she knew this was important at her company. She listed the anticipated salary as her five year goal. She kept asking herself what it would take to achieve it. She set mini-goals; complete writing and speaking courses at a bona fide college, become a regular contributor to the company newsletter; stay alert for job postings and move into an area that offers higher pay. Meg wanted to be sure she was on the right path. She contacted the Information Technology Association of America (ITAA) and learned that 52% of survey respondents (500 hiring managers participated) ranked interpersonal skills most desired by IT executives. She felt so buoyed by what she learned that she built the remainder of her plan around solid information she obtained via research. As a bonus she became an expert on her industry and this know-how was invaluable in her capacity as an Admin and kept her "on track" for reaching her five year goal.

There may be a Meg somewhere who has performed as described above. But, the Meg mentioned here is only representative of many highly motivated Admins who have shared their experiences with me.

ACTION STEPS:

- You can create your career within your current position. Maybe you don't want to move up or out of your area. Look for ways to expand your role. Take on new projects, use your creativity to make your job more interesting, and remember to look for ways to streamline processes.

- Remember, job security lies within you, not within the company.
- If you continually develop yourself, grow, and expand your talents, you will maintain marketability and have a competitive edge.
- Use every learning resource available whether it is a book, DVD or audio program, formal schooling, seminars, or the internet.

"Staying on the cutting edge; includes keeping up with technology, being willing to take risks, looking for better ways to do things, knowing what the rest of the world is doing, opening your horizons to other departments, volunteering for extra projects." (Source: my previous book, *Become An Inner Circle Assistant*).

NAVIGATING YOUR CAREER

It starts with YOU and what you want for your life – which also affects those around you such as your family.

#1 CONSIDER YOUR VALUES

Considering your values is an important step in preparing to set goals because you should not sacrifice your highest values to attain your goals. They should tie into, support and help you reach your goals as much as possible.

Activity A: Check each value that is important to you in the box to the left of the value.

☐ Leisure time____   ☐ Exciting life____

☐ Sense of ____   ☐ Recognition____
   accomplishments   by others

☐ Hard work____   ☐ Being a team player____

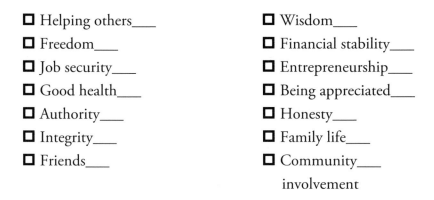

☐ Helping others____   ☐ Wisdom____
☐ Freedom____   ☐ Financial stability____
☐ Job security____   ☐ Entrepreneurship____
☐ Good health____   ☐ Being appreciated____
☐ Authority____   ☐ Honesty____
☐ Integrity____   ☐ Family life____
☐ Friends____   ☐ Community____
                               involvement

Activity B: Which of the values listed above are you willing to sacrifice occasionally? Place an "O" on the line to the right of those values. Don't hesitate to add to the list (e.g., work with positive people) and don't be concerned if you check everything. It suggests that you're a well-rounded individual. Realistically, though, sometimes values and goals may conflict. For example, you can place high value on family life, but you may have to sacrifice time with your family to achieve a professional goal. Of course there are some values, like integrity, that you should never sacrifice.

Are there *conflicting values* with which you need to come to terms? If, for example, you value your leisure time but a series of classes are to be held for the next six Saturdays and you need to learn more about new products will you: forfeit leisure time, miss an opportunity to learn more about new products? Opting to favor the learning value and return to favor your leisure time value in six weeks could seem sensible. But, if your leisure time is responsible for returning you to a busy work week refreshed and ready to perform well … it may not be negotiable. Conflicting values can pitch you a curve. Give your values serious thought and be aware that some … like integrity … are sacrosanct.

   I Value ….

Leisure time

Sense of accomplishment

Freedom

Security

Good health
Financial stability
Family life
Knowledge (of the business or new products)
Other ....

#2 ASSESSING STRENGTHS AND AREAS FOR GROWTH

Before getting into the actual process of setting and achieving goals, the next step is to identify areas of strength and areas of growth. I'm sure you've had to do something similar in your performance review or development plans. This also applies to setting goals.

Meg, mentioned in Illustration A, recognized that she needed to improve her writing skills. She tackled the challenge by attending classes but, she had options. She could have hired a personal tutor, used a computer teaching program, purchased or borrowed how-to books. With a nothing-can-stop-me-now approach, she couldn't fail.

"In order to succeed, your desire for success should be greater than your fear of failure."
—Bill Cosby. American actor, comedian and producer. B. 1937

Star assistants continually assess their strengths, use those strengths, seek areas for growth, and base professional goals on their core values.

ACTIVITY

List your personal and professional strengths. Identify areas where you need to grow.

Top 5 Strengths:

1. _____
2. _____
3. _____
4. _____
5. _____

Top 5 Weaknesses:

1. _____
2. _____
3. _____
4. _____
5. _____

Next steps:

1. <u>Use your strengths as much as you can at work</u>. These are the areas in which you naturally excel. If your work does not require you to use some of those strengths, look for opportunities outside of work until the day comes when you can apply them in your job.

2. <u>Work on areas for growth</u>. Attend classes, read books, participate at seminars and conferences, listen to CDs in the car or while jogging, and watch educational DVDs. You eventually want to be able to add those to your strength column and then add new areas for growth. This should be a never-ending process as long as you are in the workforce.

3. <u>Come back to this list every three months</u> and check where you are in your development. Add to either column and then follow steps #1 and #2 above.

#3 BELIEVE IN YOURSELF

1. Do you think people can achieve anything they set their minds to if they believe they can?

This is an important first step in reaching goals. You have to believe you can reach your goal or accomplish a task for it to happen. It's that belief that gets you through the tough times and helps you overcome barriers. Anyone who has done anything worthwhile, served others or conquered barriers knows there are difficulties along the way, but it is her belief in what she wants to do that keeps her going.

Illustration B: Aging and infirmed parents often need help from their children. According to AARP figures, the typical caregiver in the United States is a 46 year old woman. (Source: www.DiversityJobs.com – 2006). She works outside the home. Put the spotlight on Vicki. She is a wife and mother of teenage children and her mother and mother-in-law live with her and her immediate family. Vicki has an opportunity to take a new job that will boost her responsibilities and her salary but she will have to travel a few days each month. Her 5 year plan calls for "a managerial position with a staff of four or more." How can she travel with the older parents at home who need so much of her time? She decides to take the job. She reasons that with her salary increase, she can hire people to provide household assistance. This will give her more "quality time" with the older parents. Moreover, the travel demands are not great so she won't be away from home too much. She enlists assistance from her teenagers during the days she is traveling. She reminds them the increased household income will enable them to have some "extras." She follows through on the promise.

Vicki, like Meg mentioned above, is representative of the great numbers of successful Admins who have made these choices and used creativity to achieve goals. As far as Vicki was concerned she turned lemons (a possible missed opportunity) into lemonade (a map for success).

2. Do you really believe people are successful or have great professions because they are lucky?

Maybe some people are just lucky, but most aren't. People have satisfying careers and achieve wonderful things because of hard work, dedication and commitment. They reach their destinations by visualizing, planning, and learning, adjusting, networking and using mental energy. Physical stamina plays a role too.

(The Prelude to *Underneath It All* puts this aspect of success under the microscope. If you didn't read it, you may want to do so now. You could say I was unlucky. Fact is, I was slowed down but never defeated!)

3. Do you believe you can accomplish anything you desire in your career? Why or why not?

Your belief system is the catalyst to career accomplishment and personal satisfaction. It is the foundation upon which everything else builds. Your belief system has to be strong enough that doubtful peers and friends don't rattle you. Their fears and pessimism must not get in the way of making your dreams become a reality.

#4 SET GOALS

What do you want to be when you grow up? Did you answer, "I already am grown up"? You may be aging every year chronologically, but you don't ever have to grow up in terms of feeling that you can't change your mind on your course in life. You always have the opportunity to expand your horizons. There are opportunities to move up, move out or expand your current position. It's up to you.

Illustration C: Eight years ago, Susan's entire department was closed. She received 6 months severance pay.   She had worked in marketing communications and knew she wanted to become a Webmaster. She had to attend classes full-time for 9 months to sharpen skills and obtain certification. Could she afford to be without income for 3 months? She enrolled in the program and kept a tight reign on spending. Soon after she was certified she was offered a Webmaster position with a modest starting salary. She accepted the job with the proviso that she would be eligible for an increase in salary at the end of 60 days. She got the raise. Upon reflection, Susan says – "The belt-tightening period made me bolder about asking for money!" Today, Susan is widely recognized as an expert Webmaster and well paid for her services.

Susan probably forgot that she shared this experience with me but I remember all those years ago when she was trying to decide if she could "afford" to return to the classroom. I'm happy to say, I encouraged her to follow her dream.

As you walk through the steps to setting and achieving goals, keep in mind that you are learning a process. Once you learn the process, you can apply it to long- or short-term goals: personal, professional, health, social, family or spiritual.

The first step is to know what you want. Once that is determined, you will need to describe your goal in detail. If you are not exactly sure about what you want and what it will "look" like, then how will you know you achieved it? The more specific your target is, the easier it is to work toward it. It's like taking a blank canvas and already seeing the picture in detail before drawing it.

ACTIVITY: WRITE YOUR ONE-YEAR DETAILED GOAL

My Goal: _____

Details: _____

_____

_____

_____

_____

_____

WE GROW OLD BECAUSE WE STOP PLAYING

THE STORY OF ROSE

A careful search for the name of the author was unsuccessful.
Various sources present this story and "credit" the author as – Unknown.

The first day of school, our professor introduced himself and challenged us to get to know someone we didn't already know. I stood up to look around when a gentle hand touched my shoulder. I turned around to find a wrinkled, little old lady beaming up at me with a smile that lit up her entire being. She said, "Hi handsome. My name is Rose. I'm 87 years old. Can I give you a hug?"

I laughed and enthusiastically responded, "Of course you may!" and she gave me a giant squeeze. "Why are you in college at such a young, innocent age?" I asked.

She jokingly replied, "I'm here to meet a rich husband, get married, have a couple of children, and then retire and travel." "No seriously," I asked. I was curious what may have motivated her to be taking on this challenge at her age. "I always dreamed of having a college education and now I am!" she told me. After class, we walked to the student union building and shared a chocolate milkshake. We became instant friends.

Every day for the next three months we would leave class together and talk nonstop. I was always mesmerized listening to this "time machine" as she shared her wisdom and experience with me. Over the course of the year, Rose became a campus icon and easily made friends wherever she went. She loved to dress up and she reveled in the attention bestowed upon her from the other students. She was living it up. At the end of the semester, we invited Rose to speak at our football banquet and I'll never forget what she taught us.

She was introduced and stepped up to the podium. As she began to deliver her prepared speech, she dropped her three-by-five cards on the floor. Frustrated and a little embarrassed, she leaned into the microphone and simply said, "I'm sorry I'm so jittery. I gave up beer for Lent and this whiskey is killing me! I'll never get my speech back in order so let me just tell you what I know."

As we laughed, she cleared her throat and began:

"We don't stop playing because we are old; we grow old because we stop playing. There are only four secrets to staying young, being happy and achieving success:

1. You have to laugh and find humor every day.
2. You've got to have a dream. When you lose your dreams you die. We have so many people walking around who are dead and don't even know it!
3. There is a huge difference between growing older and growing up. If you are 19 years old and lie in bed for one full year and don't do one

productive thing, you will turn 20 years old. If I am 87 years old and stay in bed for a year and never do anything, I will turn 88. Anybody can grow older. That doesn't take any talent or ability. The idea is to grow up by always finding the opportunity in change.

4. Have no regrets. The elderly usually don't have regrets for what we did, but rather for things we did not do. The only people who fear death are those with regrets."

She concluded her speech by courageously singing "The Rose." She challenged each of us to study the lyrics and live them out in our daily lives. At the year's end, Rose finished the college degree she had begun all those years ago. One week after graduation, Rose died peacefully in her sleep. Over 2,000 college students attended her funeral in tribute to the wonderful woman who taught by example that it's never too late to be all you can possibly be.

#5 Write A Plan

You must write your goals and develop a specific plan for reaching them. Many people hesitate to write out their goals because they are afraid they might not achieve them. Until you write your goals, they are only partially formed dreams (i.e., they don't have shape and substance), and as long as they remain in that "place" they will not become your realities.

Rose, in the above mentioned story, gave shape and substance to her dreams. She enrolled in college and attended classes. She probably attended on winter days when she would have preferred to snuggle in front of a fireplace and read a good book or, when her grandchildren wanted to come for a visit. In the beginning, she didn't consider how she would feel about traveling to classes in cold weather or missing some time with her grandchildren. There were dozens of other things she didn't consider. These things only captured her attention as she lived out her days as a student. But she had a plan. She was determined to succeed and so nothing was going to deter her from following the plan.

ACTIVITY: TO HELP WRITE YOUR PLAN, COMPLETE THE STATEMENTS BELOW.

1. My deadline date for reaching my goal is: _____.
2. Write the tasks you need to do to reach your goal.
3. Start backtracking. Using your deadline date and the tasks above, write a monthly plan of what has to be done.
4. Go one step further. Establish weeks in which the tasks will be done. This is especially important as the time gets closer to your deadline date.

"If you do not plan where you are going, you will get sidetracked, you will get lost and you will stay longer in a place than you should.
You cannot reach a destination without a map.
You cannot reach your goals without a written plan."
—Joan Burge

#6 MONITOR YOUR PROGRESS

This is a step some people skip because they are reluctant to monitor their progress. If they don't meet deadlines or complete specific tasks, they feel overwhelmed or disappointed. This can lead to doubt, discouragement and a desire to give up.

Monitoring your progress keeps you on track and focused. You know when you have fallen behind and when you are ahead of schedule. There is nothing wrong with falling behind as long as you set a new deadline date for completing that particular task.

Here are some steps you can take to monitor your progress.

1. Keep a hard copy of your list of tasks and deadline dates so you can more easily follow up on them. While there are many software programs that will help you track your progress through "follow-up" reminders that pop up on your computer screen, a hard copy you view regularly is your best bet.

2. At least once a week, mark the status of each task.

3. If you completed the task, mark it as such. Good job!

4. If you did not complete the task, write a new deadline date.

5. If necessary, add tasks to the list and delete tasks that aren't necessary.

6. Stay with it. It's easy to give up after a few weeks or months. It takes real dedication and commitment to stay on task and monitor your progress.

7. Some people give themselves small rewards when tasks are completed. It can be as basic as a twenty minute block of unscheduled time! Reward yourself if you choose. Why not? (More about rewards to follow.)

#7 USE RESOURCES EFFECTIVELY

It can be lonely and difficult to accomplish goals on your own. It's certainly not as much fun as involving others. You need others for their expertise, guidance, knowledge, support and inspiration. (At the same time, if you're committed to achieve a goal and don't find support in your immediate circle don't despair. When people see you perform and know that you "mean it" … they may react differently. If not, keep going. Whose life is it anyway?)

Communicate. Share your dream with a friend, family member, peer or professional associate and let that person know you're "open" for suggestions. Ask people who know about your plan to recommend resources or contacts. Nuture these "relationships" and you may develop a never-ending source of helpful information.

Use Mentors. Find people who have done what you want to do, or have what you want to have. You'll be able to sincerely compliment them about their achievements. Ask how they overcame barriers. Mentors can help you solve problems. Sometimes you've got the solution in-mind, but don't know it until you hear yourself say it aloud to a mentor.

Conduct Research. You have numerous resources available today – everything from people contacts to the information highway.

#8 Reward Yourself

Consider rewarding yourself for your achievements. Your reward can be something little or big. Establish your reward at the time you write your goal. You can also have mini-rewards along the way.

The following reward shall be mine when I reach my goal:

_____

_____

_____

#9 Commit To Your Goal

Personal commitment is extremely important to staying motivated when you feel discouraged. Many times, this is what makes the difference between people who achieve their goals and people who stay in their comfort zones and never grow. Commitment is taking ownership and responsibility.

Commitment comes in many forms. It is…

- doing what you don't really feel like doing, but know you must
- knowing when to say -- no
- sacrificing "play" time for "work" time
- wanting to give up because that would be the easiest thing in the world to do, but you don't
- faith and perseverance, like parenting... it never stops

#10 Desire For Reaching Your Goal

Along with commitment comes desire. A strong desire to reach your goal is a key to success. When you set your goal, think about how strongly you want to reach it. Measure your desire on a scale of 1 to 10. Can you see yourself reaching that goal? Can you see how life might change as a result? How strong is your desire to accomplish something or be in a certain position? If your desire rates 6 or below you should reconsider working toward that goal. Maybe you don't want it as badly as you think you do. Instead, put your energies into goals where your desire is at least a 7 or above. Your chances for success are much higher.

#11 Recognize Opportunities for Growth

Sometimes "barriers" or "roadblocks" are actually opportunities for growth. As you chart your course and set out to reach a goal, you'll encounter barriers. At that point, you have a choice: Turn around, crawl into your comfort zone and give up, or you find ways to get around the barriers. Use them as learning experiences. If you choose the second, and I hope you will, you will learn more than you ever would by having everything go smoothly. Barriers are only challenges. They are tests of how true you are to your dreams.

Can you predict what barriers you might encounter along the way? Finances might be an obstacle. A person at work, your spouse or parents can serve as a barrier. Once you anticipate possible barriers, you can write a plan for overcoming them. This puts you in a proactive position; you are in control, not the roadblock.

ARE YOU ACHIEVING YOUR GOALS?

ACTIVITY: COMPLETE THE CHART BELOW TO THE BEST OF YOUR ABILITY.

EXPLANATIONS:

Rating: in terms of importance to other goals listed.

Energy Level: when you think of the goal, does your energy level increase or decrease?

Blocking Beliefs: list any current or old beliefs related to that goal that could prevent you from achieving it.

GOAL (CAREER, PERSONAL, FAMILY)	RATING IMPORTANCE	ENERGY LEVEL (INCREASE/DECREASE)	BLOCKING BELIEFS

Note: This chart can help you when you have 3 or more goals because 1) it helps you prioritize, 2) you'll see which ones really motivate you, and 3) you will have identified barriers created in your mind.

BREAK THROUGH A CAREER PLATEAU – AND CLIMB TO THE STARS!

Employees often ask me "How can I continue advancing my career after I feel I've hit a job plateau?" They also tell me that they like who they work for and the work they do, but feel stagnant. Anyone who asks that question is a go-getter! How does an employee continue moving forward in her chosen profession?

Expand your job. A lull in your career may signal you're ready for new challenges – not necessarily a new job. So broaden the scope of the work you do: Look for projects that highlight your particular strengths – tasks that step beyond your job description, but that you feel qualified doing or learning. The reason is when advancing your career, the skills you've demonstrated are often more important than the title you've held. Doing higher-level, more complicated work will expand your skill set and earn you kudos and new opportunities in the process.

Illustration D: Mimi's new boss was a micro-manager. Little by little, he reduced Mimi's responsibilities. After about 6 months Mimi started to think about quitting her job. "I'm so bored," she lamented to her sister.

Her sister worked in another department and knew a lot about the company. "Why don't you ask if you can oversee the Scholarship Program?" she offered. The company had an admirable program and the man who was in charge of it had been promoted and hadn't named a successor. Mimi agreed it was a good idea. *I don't think this responsibility will work against my supervisor… I bet he'll go for it.* Four weeks later, Mimi was officially named the contact person for the company scholarship program. Later, her supervisor acted as though the whole thing was his idea. He cooperated with Mimi fully. *"Are you sure you don't need more time to devote to this job?"* he asked from time to time. Eventually, Mimi posted for another position in the company and no longer inter-acted with this executive. While she waited for an opportunity to present itself; she got busy with something new and rewarding.

There is a Mimi who oversees a scholarship program in a utility company but as to whether she has a sister, I do not know. I do know other Admins have used this strategy successfully.

Seek new education or training. When you feel your career is in a rut, try to find educational opportunities that re-ignite your curiosity about the world – and inspire you to achieve even more. Whether you pursue formal schooling or seek professional training through conferences and seminars, you're sure to benefit, and so is your career.

Ask for guidance. Perhaps there's a barrier to advancing that you can't see. Or maybe there's an obvious way to move forward – but it's not immediately evident to you. In either case, when you feel stymied, seek the advice of someone you trust – someone who understands your career aspirations. It could be your supervisor, a mentor, an HR manager or even a career coach.

Speak up. Career stagnation can sometimes be fixed by speaking frankly to your manager about the situation. Make no assumptions! If managers are unaware of your views, then you haven't given them the opportunity to help you identify new ways to grow and expand your career.

Move on. Of course, if none of the above suggestions work, you may want to consider whether there's another job that suits you better – one that's more in line with your future career goals. Write down all the pros and cons to keeping your current position. If the cons outweigh the pros, have the courage of your convictions to begin seeking a new position.

ALIGN YOUR PROFESSIONAL GOALS WITH YOUR EMPLOYER'S GOALS

For the past several years, progressive organizations require administrative professionals to align their goals with their department and company goals. This trend is gaining popularity because executives discover that when every person in the company is *on the same page* overall success increases and everyone benefits.

What if this progressive approach to *alignment* doesn't ring any bells in your organization? And, what if there's never company leadership in this direction? Can you, nevertheless, align yourself with company goals? Should you?

Yes, you can.

Yes, you should.

Here's why – YOU:

- Use your energies on tasks and projects that actually make a difference or have impact on the bottom line.
- Experience personal satisfaction because you *feel* like an integral part of the department or organization. Who doesn't like to feel like she is part of success?
- You are perceived as someone who knows what *is* going on.
- You are working in tandem with the people who make a difference in your organization.

- It can lead to mid-year salary increases or higher % of annual increases. (If the norm for increases is 3.9%, you may receive a 4% or 4.5% increase).
- Career advancement is practically guaranteed.
- You are respected as a key business partner with upper management.

The activity below is one I use in my World Class Assistant™ Certificate program. Approximately 60% of the attendees have a difficult time completing this assignment. See how well you do.

DEPARTMENT:

a. My department's goals for this year are:

b. The professional goals I have that I can align with those goals are:

ORGANIZATION:

a. My organization's goals for this year are:

b. The professional goals I have that I can align with those goals are:

BONUS: You get 3 stars if you can answer this.

My company's mission statement is:

How do I *fit in* (or, align) with the company's mission?

Our company's values are:

What skills, attitudes and behaviors do I have (or need to develop) to *snuggle up* to my company's values?

Example of values:
innovation
customer service
team work
quality performance
leadership

WHAT NEXT?

1. Blend *alignment* into your organizational development plans, if possible.
2. Monitor progress. Come back to this page in three, six and nine months. How am I doing?
3. Use this activity sheet unless or until you can make the assessment process better. After all, if you're on the fast track for growth and development, it follows that you will find ways to improve analysis.

> *"However beautiful the strategy, you should occasionally look at the results."*
> —Winston Churchill, British orator, author and Prime Minister 1874 -1965

CREATING YOUR CAREER PORTFOLIO

Why would it be beneficial to create a Career Portfolio?
- Demonstrates you take pride in achievements
- Shows you are proactive

- A permanent record isn't subject to the vagaries of memory
- Delivers the message; *If I did it once … I can do it again*
- Your "industry" makes you worthy of higher levels of recognition
- Shows your creativity

When and where you can use it?
- During your performance review
- When writing your professional development plan for the upcoming year and tracking accomplishments
- While competing for an internal job
- When a new boss comes on board and you want him or her to quickly gain an overview of your talents and experiences
- Asking for additional responsibility
- Outside work – if you are trying to obtain a leadership role
- When being considered for committee work
- External interviewing

What can you put into this portfolio? Many things, but here are some suggestions:
- Professional photo of yourself (no larger than 4 x 6 in.)
- Record of any outside work; volunteer or committee work
- Thank-you notes from customers or clients on a job well done
- Thank-you letters from other divisions or executives on a job well done
- Examples of your work: graphic work, spreadsheets (<u>do not</u> divulge confidential employer information)
- Past evaluations (not more than three years old)
- Your mission statement and vision
- Customer appreciation letters

- Resume (have extra copies in the back pocket if you use a three-ring binder)
- Emphasize results and accomplishments vs. job duties!
- Copies of Certificates of Completion

Extras could include a table of contents, cover letter and an informational CD! <u>Note</u>: Do not leave this portfolio with the interviewer or others reviewing your portfolio. That is why you might want to leave a copy of a CD, and have extra copies of your most recent resume and cover letter.

Place these in a nice leather portfolio, possibly with your initials on it. Or you might want to use a three-ring binder. Be creative. Remember, the outside packaging also represents you and will send a message to the person viewing your portfolio. Think: clean lines… professional looking with quality samples of your work. Also think about the font style and size, as well as the color paper you will use; again, keep it professional. You might want to use some nice sheet protectors as well.

PREPARING FOR YOUR PERFORMANCE REVIEW

Last minute preparation is out of the question!

Fact is, from the moment you're hired you're subject to evaluation. So, use everyday as a day to favorably influence the assessment that formally comes once or twice a year. When the official Review is on the calendar consider the following:

1A. Anticipate the reviewer – what does he or she *want from you*? Answer this question now and it's easier to get ready for a face-to-face meeting. *Note: if the reviewer is your supervisor, your answers will probably be slightly different than if the reviewer is the Human Resources manager. You can be more "specific" with your supervisor who is more likely to appreciate details that would only confound the HR manager.* This is the time to review any notes you made after your last Performance Review.

What does the Reviewer *want from you?*

- A formal demeanor and good manners
- Answers that are short and to the point
- No excuses. Instead, present fact-focused explanations:
  - The final figures weren't available until after 5:00 PM on Mondays in May. That's why the reports weren't delivered before Tuesday afternoons.
  - A snow storm in Altoona delayed all flights. The custom-printer-cartridges weren't off-loaded from the plane for almost 24 hours. We had no reason to believe our supplier wasn't telling the truth about delivery time but this confidence came back to bite us. We would have outsourced the printing if we had reliable information. Our printed announcements arrived at the convention center too late to be distributed.
- The illustration just discussed underscores candor! Perfection is only a notion. Printer cartridges that arrived too late to be useful probably should be mentioned. Don't purposely try to introduce "negatives" but don't ignore them either.
- Sensible questions. Don't ask questions this reviewer probably can't answer or questions that don't serve a purpose.
- Demonstrate you care about the company. Mention something the industry association reports, for example, and ask how it will impact your company.
- Sincerity. "I don't know but I'll find out," is a better response than attempting to be a know-it-all. Your willingness to expose your vulnerability helps establish your honesty.
- Improvement strategies. How can you make yourself more valuable to the company? Tell the reviewer you'll do so and how

you'll proceed. The reviewer usually needs this information in order to conclude the assignment.

1B. Performance Reviews almost always focus on money. Will you get a salary increase? How about a bonus? Will this be on hold until the next review? It's helpful if you realize that during a Performance Review, you're the salesperson and the product is YOU. A competent sales person is usually happy with the outcome.

- Listen to the reviewer carefully
- Don't say more than necessary
- This is no time for modesty ... speak about achievements (e.g., saved the company money)
- Think about how you'll respond if you are disappointed by the amount of the salary increase or other monetary offers. A good sales person knows that everything is negotiable. You may want to set the stage now for next time.
- Maintain composure, don't show anger. Demonstrate professionalism no matter what.

2. Amy Maxson, a Wisconsin-based career coach, calls them Proactive Performance Reviews – be involved before, during, and after your review! I like the way Ms. Maxson *compartmentalizes* and immediately thought of the steps that follow. Feel free to add steps of your own and see whether you like this BEFORE, DURING, AFTER approach.

BEFORE

- Okay, so you're good at your job! Collect supporting information. These may include: thank you notes from customers or clients. E-mail notes are acceptable. Print copies and file them.

- Maintain a Summary of Achievements. This may include: seminar attendance dates, titles and personal observations about what you learned. Chamber of Commerce professional organization meetings you attended as a representative for your executive and/or the company. List personal (e.g., I learned how to speak Spanish and professional achievements (e.g., I hired two employees and they are an asset to the department.) You may want to close your Summary with a "best of the year" list. It should draw the reader's attention and help to quickly make your point.

- Present everything you assemble in a good looking folder or 3 ring binder. Remember appearances count. A simple Table of Contents helps to maintain order. Color-coded pages are attractive and help categorize topics. Be creative. Include a recent photo. Remember, this "tool" speaks for you.

DURING

- Of course, you'll come to work that day especially well dressed and groomed. Don't forget to shine your shoes!

- Be aware of your body language. Smile. Maintain eye-contact. Remember if you grimace when you hear something you don't like … the reviewer gets the message loud and clear. That may not be to your advantage.

- Be aware of the reviewer's body language too. Can you read it? You may pick up a useful tip. For example, if the individual leans forward, it could be you're speaking too softly. A soft spoken individual is sometimes perceived to lack confidence. Raise your voice slightly and you may see the reviewer lean back.

AFTER

- Record your impressions:
    - o   I should have said ….
    - o   I should not have said …
- Relax. Congratulate yourself if results please you. If they don't please you, relax anyway. You'll be better prepared to tweak your plans when you're rested.
- Think of all the ways you can use the information you obtained. For example, do you want to leave this company? You may now possess sufficient information to make a final decision.
- Consult with your mentor.   If you share some of this experience – your mentor may "see" something you didn't consider.
- Put this review into the *history books*. But, before you do … try to select at least two things you can begin to use now to prepare for next time.

GENERAL TIPS:

Be on time.

Bring samples of work you have done.

Don't be negative.

Don't slouch.

Be open; not rigid in your ways or attitudes.

Ask for clarification if you do not understand the ratings your manager gave you.

Ask your manager, "What can I do to get a higher rating next time?"

A Unique Bonus Tip: Jasmine Freeman really surprised me when she knew she was going to have her first Review with me. She contacted Dawn, a former assistant of mine, to ask for help.

(That was a genius thing to do! But, there's more!)

I conduct a very in-depth performance review because it's so closely aligned with my work. (Practice what you preach!) I put Dawn through five pages of questions. I got to thinking it was Jasmine's first review and she was hired when everything at the office was in a spin so maybe I won't be so intense this time.

We went to lunch to discuss her performance. Since Jasmine met with my former assistant, she came prepared with a five page questionnaire; all typed with her answers and observations and handed it to me. (Wouldn't you be surprised?)

Jasmine demonstrated her initiative; showed she was a creative researcher and not shy about going the extra mile to achieve a goal. She anticipated, prepared and strategically positioned herself for the review. Clearly, Jasmine wanted to excel at her job and that is what I wanted too.

NEW APPROACH TO RESUME WRITING

Since it's possible that a computer will read your resume before it is given serious consideration by a homo sapien ... by all means; write it for a computer.

If you're asked to fill out a computer job application, one expert source refers to it as a resume in disguise. (Source: http://www.pueblo.gsa.gov). Note: This is an excellent source for detailed information about resumes, applications, and cover letters.

For the electronic world, you're advised to use keywords and simple formats. Boldface and bullets aren't appropriate. The most important information comes before the least important information albeit all of it should be relevant.

Some key points are briefly mentioned below but you are best served by reading up-to-the-minute articles and books that are exclusively devoted to this topic.

— ⋅⊹⋅ ———— ⋅⟨⋅⟩⋅ ———— ⋅⊹⋅ —

Focus on outcomes/results: Your goal is to communicate your abilities. What better way to get the message across than to focus on outcomes/results?

Sample Set Up for Resume

Your mission or objective: What do you want?

Overview of your career/work history: This is where you list the typical tasks assistants are expected to perform

Career Highlights: List each employer and what you did above and beyond in that job; or tasks you performed that you did not perform in other jobs. This shows them you have a diverse background. Use strong action verbs to start each sentence.

Education

Additional training and certifications: Outside Work Interests – list associations and community work you are involved in that helps you demonstrate leadership and organizational skills.

REALIZING YOUR FULL POTENTIAL: VENTURING INTO HIGH SEAS

In life we are either adventurers riding the high seas or drifters just floating along. One is not better than the other; we need to just "float" sometimes and enjoy the scenery. Riding the high seas is where we really have an opportunity to grow. That is because adventurers will. . .

- reach out to people they would otherwise not engage

67

- use their creativity and be resourceful
- notice things they don't see in calm waters
- "muster up" every bit of strength
- be invigorated – *come alive*
- and display courage

High seas can come in the form of

changes at work

dealing with personal challenges and balancing work

taking on a major assignment or project

an exciting new administrative position

picking up your family and moving to a new place

leaving the administrative profession after many years in the field

When the Heat Is On! (It's the real test of one's ability and talent).

When I do one-on-one consulting, I often see an assistant who is a really great assistant. However, when the heat is on high, this person loses focus, neglects to prioritize, forgets things, or permits follow-up items to fall through the cracks.

Although it takes considerable talent to be a top Admin and there are large numbers of people who fill those shoes; how many among them can handle a full-blown crisis? More importantly, can you handle a full-blown crisis?

You can if you:

- remain calm
  - o If you panic you waste valuable time.
- stay focused. The tendency to race ahead and envision a dreadful outcome is strong. You can't do that if you stay focused. And, that's just for starters!

- think – weigh pros and cons
- name your options. Did you leave out anything? Which is most likely to succeed?
    - act decisively
- don't second-guess yourself

Illustration: An Admin named Carla was the first to realize the office safe was missing. "How could this be?" she shouted.   The safe had been in the usual place when she arrived in the morning. She knew it contained Top Secret files her partner had been working on.   It was a large and heavy safe and couldn't possibly be removed without someone seeing something.   She realized her hands were shaking.   She sat down and took a few deep breaths and considered what to do next.   The executive she supported was out of town for the day.   Should she contact him?   Should she call the police? Should she wait for tomorrow when he would be in the office?   Should she tell someone?   She decided that if a robbery had occurred it was best to investigate as soon as possible.   She must not wait for tomorrow.   She realized her manager was currently in flight and wouldn't be able to receive a phone call.   She had another option.   Call the company CEO.   He was based in Washington, DC.   She called and refused to speak to anyone but him. She explained the situation and he told her he would call the authorities. Within minutes, people from the FBI were in her office.   She was still shaking when she went home that evening.   She sipped a glass of wine and reflected on her actions.   She was content that she had acted appropriately. Later that week, the CEO mailed a letter of commendation to her.   He commented on her quick and intelligent response.   She never did learn if the safe was recovered or if the Top Secret files were compromised.   But she did know that she could handle an emergency situation well.   She didn't have to guess how she would react if … she had her "if" and she was equal to it.

The Carla who telephoned the company CEO in Washington isn't a Carla I know. To me, she is a composite of dozens of very smart and unshakable Admins who do the right things when faced with emergency situations!

UNDERNEATH IT ALL

You really need to know yourself. I covered this briefly in *Become An Inner Circle Assistant – Know Thyself* – but this time we're going deeper. It's knowing who you are deep inside and having the courage to use that information to live the life you want.

- This does not mean you ignore others or are selfish.

- It means you are *self-actualized*. Therefore, everything you do you do better than before you awoke to this realization and put it to work for you.

- You want to do more, give more, help others, and you have more energy to do so.

MASLOW'S HEIRACHY OF NEEDS

Psychology students are only some of the people who are familiar with Abraham Maslow and his great body of work related to human beings and what makes them thrive (or, wither). Maslow describes self-actualization as a person's need to be and do that which the person was "born to do." (Source: http://honolulu.hawaii.edu).

Another way to express this is …

- The instinctual need of humans to make the most of their abilities and to strive to be the best they can be.

- The desire to realize all of his potential for being an effective, creative, mature human being. "What a man can be, he must be …"

    (Source: http://en.wikipedia.org).

It would be inappropriate to attempt to "boil down" Maslow's findings into a few paragraphs but it would be a serious omission to not mention his contribution to our understanding of what makes us tick!

(If you really want to get Underneath It All in this area, I urge you to read detailed articles and books that discuss MASLOW'S HEIRARCHY OF NEEDS.)

What would Maslow (who was born in 1908) tell today's administrative professionals about their needs? We operate in time-compressed environments. We're involved in a multitude of things; 40 – 50 hour work weeks, taking extra classes (live or on-line) in the evenings to maintain a competitive edge, caring for aging parents, being involved in professional organizations, raising our children and sometimes, involvement with raising our grandchildren.

Could it be that *now more than ever* you have to do work that feeds your soul and mind? As far as I'm concerned … that's an affirmative!

You will hit road blocks – barriers and sometimes monumental barriers like I did with Dave's cancer. There were times I thought, "My dreams, goals, and work aren't important." "Nothing matters other than Dave's wellness." Then I would realize life will go on and I still want to accomplish certain things. Those dreams or goals were just put on the back burner for awhile – a rather long while (2½ years because of my own surgery prior to Dave's situation.)

Time is precious and you need to make a decision as to what you want to do with your life. To lift yourself to new heights you have to make tough decisions, say "no" more often, and be selective.

Four

"Professionalism" Works for Me

People decide to like you, trust you, do business with you all because you impress them. You make them feel safe and comfortable. They believe goals shall be accomplished in your capable hands. People who like you are usually eager to please you too.

How do you earn this enviable status?

You must look and act *the part*. In short, you groom yourself to be the consummate professional.

Times change – You Change

Illustration. Mary worked for the ABC Company for 20 years. She started in a typing pool and eventually was promoted to work with a company vice president. She was Dan Darcy's right-hand person. There was a time when everyone knew Mary but that was no longer the case. The company prospered and now more than half the employees were recent hires. When people formed "first impressions" about Mary she got dubbed as old-fashioned and out of touch. Her hairstyle hadn't changed for at least a decade. She wore only dark pant suits to the office and she wasn't aware of the popular television show, American Idol, didn't know anything about text messaging or blogs or the topics people tend to discuss. "Old fashioned" is not a trademark that benefits Mary or Mr. Darcy!

I don't know this particular Mary. She is strictly a "model" for some *Admins* who think they can *rest on their laurels*. The Mary's and Marty's in offices around the country diminish their effectiveness when they don't change and grow with the times.

> *"Time changes everything except something within us which*
> *is always surprised by change."*
> —Thomas Hardy, British novelist and poet. 1840-1928

DOES YOUR PERSONAL APPEARANCE SPEAK WELL FOR YOU?

Some highly successful *Admins* create a signature trademark apropos their wardrobe, hair style, posture and even their body language (e.g. smiles, handshakes).

(Note: Your trademark is something by which you come to be known. Or, as mentioned in "The American Heritage® Dictionary of the English Language, Fourth edition …A distinctive characteristic by which a person or thing comes to be known: the shuffle and snicker that became the comedian's trademark.")

You, for example, may be known for your beautiful silk blouses, your firm handshake and quick smile. *These things go to the office with you everyday* … rain or shine … good days or difficult days. People can always count on you to wear a beautiful blouse, extend your hand (when appropriate) for a firm handshake and to greet them with a quick smile! Without saying a word you establish a certain air of dependability and that's a welcome attribute!

YOU ARE ON STAGE!

Everyday, as soon as you walk into the office, you are on stage. When you walk into someone's office, down the hall, into another department – you are on stage. You're also on stage when you speak to someone on the telephone or send e-mail. Although they can't "eye" you, they form impressions (e.g., you have an excellent command of language; you're courteous and don't "talk over them" – your written communication is "friendly" but focused.)

PERCEPTION MANAGEMENT

Experts tell us it only takes 30 seconds for people to form an impression about us. Clearly that "first" impression carries weight. But, so does the second, third, fourth … you get the idea. When we perform in a consistent manner and establish a professional trademark we easily "manage" what others think. *That first excellent impression wasn't a fluke!* At the same time, quick impressions can be lasting impressions. Psychologists gave the phenomenon a name; the "Halo Effect."

When your visual message is positive, people assume other things about you are equally positive. If I see someone who is neatly-groomed and organized, I assume that person takes pride in how her work area looks and that she is well organized. If someone looks messy, unkempt, and scattered, I assume that applies to other things this person handles. (Unfair? Probably. Still, this response is predictable.)

BUSINESS IS LIKE A GAME; A VERY SERIOUS GAME.

Are you a major-league player? Football players and basketball players wear uniforms when they are playing their game; also a serious game to them. Why do cheerleaders wear uniforms? It sets them apart and enhances performance.

Describe your work uniform. Of course, it's not a uniform in so far as a dictionary definition is concerned but it may help if you think of it as a "true" uniform. Ask what is the "look" I want to project – traditional, classic, edgy or contemporary, classic with a little artistic look? When you are in the *game of business*, you must take your appearance seriously.

Express a look that attracts success to you – a person's outer appearance can be a distraction. Others cannot hear what you have to say when your physical appearance disturbs or distracts their focus.

You can find *that* look!

> *"Success is achieved by developing our strengths, not by eliminating our weaknesses."*
> —Marilyn vos Savant, Journalist, Columnist of Ask Marilyn. B. 1946

(Note: Did you know help is available via people who are Image Consultants? More about this later.)

YOUR PROFESSIONAL TRADEMARK – THE BIGGER PICTURE

I like everything to be coordinated. All of our Office Dynamics products have a certain look and color scheme. Our corporate colors are carried through on all our brochures and other promotional materials. That is part of our trademark.

An assistant's trademark could be that he or she is always organized and meticulous about the quality of work he or she produces.

1. Challenge yourself to list 5 items you can incorporate into your professional trademark.

    1.

    2.

    3.

    4.

    5.

2. Which of the 5 are already "working" for you? (e.g., I'm a stylish dresser. I've got outstanding posture. People often ask if I'm a yoga instructor.)

3. What would you like to be known for in so far as your professional trademark is concerned? (e.g., a strict *gatekeeper* who watches out for my executive's interests. Someone who doesn't gossip. Someone who will keep a secret). Why?

    This isn't a frivolous question. Some impressions you establish can make your work life easier! If, for example, you don't gossip … people don't waste your time or test your patience by trying to share gossip with you. While you're drafting your professional image, why not include "qualities" that send valuable messages like this one?

THE POWER OF PROFESSIONALISM

ACTIVITY: WHAT IS THE VALUE YOU WOULD DERIVE FROM PROJECTING A PROFESSIONAL IMAGE?

_____

_____

_____

_____

_____

_____

Possible answers include:

- Gain respect
- Have an immediate advantage in dealing with suppliers (e.g., vendors happily cooperate)
- Setting the *tone* with the customer right away
- Credibility
- Trust
- What I do trickles down to other staff members making it easier for me to lead
- Allows me to do the job
- It makes me feel good
- I'll leave my office at the end of the day feeling less weary and have more energy to expend on my life away from work
- Return business

YOU'VE GOT THE POWER!

- Positions you as someone with authority; hidden power; someone who must know what they are doing.
- Opportunities will open to you that will not be presented to others.
- Win-win situations occur. You become credible and people want to do business with you.
- Energy radiates from you. You feel good about yourself and others can see it/feel it.

- Desired Results are achieved.

THE RULE OF 12

I don't know who to thank for this Rule. Someone brought it to my attention years ago and I appreciate the wisdom of it all and have shared it with others. If you are the "author" or you know who the author is please contact me. I shall gladly give the author the proper credit when I refer to this Rule in the future.

Generally, people notice and begin to "size up" others at a distance of 12 feet. A good example of this is when someone enters a room… or you're mingling at a business function, but are only aware of those in your immediate vicinity.

Once you've made an initial impact on people, they'll start focusing on the **top 12 inches** of your body – specifically your face and facial expressions.

Then, whatever perception you've given them is reinforced or diminished by the **first 12 words** you speak. At this point, you've made your crucial first impression, and people will decide whether to get to know you better or not.

People's perceptions of you can be changed, of course – but it's harder to do that than making a great impression from the start of your work relationship.

Illustration: Barbara represented the executive she supported at various gatherings in the tri-state area where their company conducted business. She could usually predict whether attendees would be warm and welcoming or more reserved and stand-offish. It had as much to do with the sponsoring organization (e.g., Chamber of Commerce or real estate agents) as with the region (e.g., large cities or small towns in the North). She concentrated on looking good, sounding good, distributing business cards, and speaking to everyone in attendance when that was practical. For years she varied her wardrobe and style in an attempt to "fit in." One day she decided to simply perfect herself and put her best foot forward (the same foot) each and every time. She realized The Rule of 12 didn't need to be tweaked. This realization saved time and minimized apprehension. By concentrating on improving her posture, speaking more slowly, increasing her spoken vocabulary, remembering to smile more often she would be a "winner" wherever she went.

> *"I see left-handers a little better [than right-handers], … But I don't change anything. I still just try to see the ball and hit the ball."*
> —Yadier Molina, Cardinals (Major League) ballplayer. Born: 1982

THE POWER OF CONGRUENCY

As you can see from the Rule of 12, your outer image needs to match your spoken image. In other words, some people may look very professional on the outside, but when they open their mouths to speak, they do not sound professional. Vice versa: People who look like they just rolled out of bed may actually seem very intelligent when they speak to you. To project the most powerful image in the workplace, you want to strive for congruency, whether you are in casual business clothes or a business suit.

PROFESSIONALISM –

> *"Key players in the corporate arena are masters of communication and corporate vision. The truly successful are aware that everything about their personal presentation and their corporate trappings must be coordinated and polished to project a message of congruency."* – Gloria Starr, Image Consultant

Professionalism is:

1. Knowing your job inside and out.
2. Learning and improving the core competencies of your trade.
3. Taking time to do things right the first time.
5. Not getting emotionally involved.
6. Setting high standards for others to follow.
7. Contributing ideas to your organization or department.
8. Walking *your talk*.
9. And looking professional.

HOW DO YOU GET IT?

Observe – key people in your organization
Mirror – actions and behaviors you like in others; but don't be a clone
Learn – we have every tool available today. It's really a matter of desire,
commitment and making the time.
Practice – the areas in which you want to come across as polished.
Put Your Signature On It!

We're not talking exclusively about a pen and ink signature although that's a good place to begin …

1. Do you have a preset signature on e-mails you originate? If not, you can create one and if you already have one … critique it. Can it better represent you, your image, all that you're trying to project? You can design your signing-off signature using the font that sends the message you wish to convey. For example, the Times New Roman font is a little stiff while the Coronet font is personal and sophisticated. Did you include your job title, all phone contact numbers and the company's slogan? Should you? Ask yourself what

purpose is being served. Remember, you're in control and you can use colors, sizes, shapes, words, pictures to send a message about YOU … who you are; what you stand for and what people can expect from you. Lest you think this is a frivolous pursuit consider how much you are affected by colors. The next time you're in a food market take note of package colors. Blue, for example, implies cleanliness and purity. Red communicates power and vitality. Color is a powerful tool. Marketers pay careful attention to how it helps them do their jobs. You can do the same.

2. MORE about color. Open your closet to see which color dominates your wardrobe. Is the dominate color selected purposely or did it earn this status without your notice? Notice! What messages are you sending each day when you dress for the office? Learn all you can from books. Check your local library or book store for titles. "ColorSmart: How to Use Color to Enhance Your Business and Personal Life" by Mimi Cooper and Arlene Modica Matthews reports on several ways color impacts success. There's even a story about a woman who failed to win "the job of her dreams" until she stopped wearing her Kelly green suit and presented herself in a navy blue two piece outfit.

3. What about the color gray? Should you wear gray clothing to the office? According to the Color Marketing Group … "color sells and the right colors sell better." (See: http://www.colormarketing.org). Moreover, colors have meanings. You may soon begin to wonder how you could possibly have made it this far without possessing considerable *color smarts*!

4. *It ain't what you say.* What do you say? Do you vary your vocabulary? Do you repeat "pet" phrases too often (e.g. a sorry sight, it's not over until the fat lady sings)? **How you say what you say** impacts your image. Too verbose? Especially soft spoken? Any of

the less desirable habits you have embraced tend to shoot you in the foot where perfecting your professional signature is involved.

"While Professionalism is seen by the outside world and can be considered external, it's really a mind set. It's an internal desire to be the best one can be and give the best internal and external customer service!"
—Joan Burge

(Note: There's no shortage of books and magazines devoted to …. *Your looks.* Check libraries, scan book store shelves and magazine stands and even ask questions on-line (e.g., www.google.com – what can I do to make my hair look healthy?). Most of the time you'll find useful answers. Once you have an enviable professional signature, you'll want to maintain it. Consulting up-to-date resources will keep you at the top of your game. See: the Resources section at the end of *Underneath It All* but, don't stop there.)

General Guidelines:
1. Dress appropriately for your line of work, career goals, geographic location and body type.
2. Consistency is important.
3. Use colors that enhance your natural hair, skin, and eye coloring.
4. Dress with intent!
5. You don't have to spend a lot of money. It's a matter of *pulling your look together* and wearing clothing that works well with your body frame/shape.
6. Stay clear of trendy clothes for work.
7. Perfume is acceptable. Just don't overdose!
8. Women need to consider length and body coverage of their clothing.

9. Accessories should **enhance** your appearance, not be a **distraction** to your appearance (e.g., bracelets that jingle and over-sized earrings that swing).

10. Learn to control your *emotional state* when getting dressed.

11. Play up your positive physical attributes.

12. Take care of yourself! I'm not a health expert but most of us know that sufficient rest and exercise help us to look and perform well.

13. Few among us need to be reminded about diet. Still, to omit it would appear to be an oversight. The food and drink you ingest impacts your physical and mental well being.

And there is more:

- Keep your shoes in good condition (heels should be in good repair).
- Your hair should be clean and neatly-styled.
- Nails should be clean; for women, not too long.
- Carry a nice leather portfolio and pen to meetings.

Casual Casualties! (According to several Image Consultants)

- Too Anything! (Too much make up, too much body piercing, too many tattoos, too much jewelry, too tight, too short, too skimpy, too low, too many patterns, too frilly, too colorful.)
- Shirttail out
- Wrinkled clothes
- Unkempt hair
- Hems that need stitching
- Missing buttons
- Scuffed shoes
- Political or cause-related T-shirts; humorous attire or accessories
- "Underwear is not Outerwear"

- Shorts or Capri pants
- Tank tops or sleeveless shirts; halter tops
- Flip-flops, sandals, dirty sneakers
- Jogging suits, warm-ups, wind suits
- Poorly coordinated outfits
- Going without hosiery or socks
- No *see-through* clothing
- Undergarments that don't provide support

"To be successful today, a person must be able to dress casually and still exude as much power, credibility, and authority as when wearing a traditional business suit. Your choices of dress-down attire reflect directly your respect for your workplace, your career goals, and your level of overall professionalism."
—Sherry Maysonave

PERSONAL PACKAGING/SELF-PRESENTATION

Example:

My Current Image	My New Image
Fun	Focused
Sexy	Charismatic
Playful	Confident
Relaxed	Dynamic

List 4 adjectives that apply to your Current Image and 4 for the New Image you want to reflect.

MY CURRENT IMAGE

MY NEW IMAGE

I will make the following enhancements to my appearance:

Work area: IS AN EXTENSION OF YOU AND IT SENDS A NON-VERBAL MESSAGE. *What is it saying?* I'm here to do business and be engaged in the business OR I'm all about fun, stuffed animals and thinking about everything but work!

"Spring cleaning doesn't have to be a dreaded list of chores. It can be a rewarding experience that helps provide some structure and organization in your life."
—Peter Walsh

YOUR ORGANIZATION'S IMAGE:

What words would you use to describe the image your organization wants to project? (Examples: efficient, well-informed, enthusiastic, positive)

Does the image you project match that of your organizations?

Illustration: Marie was so well organized that her co-workers teased her about having another life as an army sergeant. She responded; let's see if you're sergeant material. I'm willing to put you through your paces. Some people made changes but eventually resumed their messy habits. The executive she supported frequently complimented her on maintaining order. "No clutter … I like that." Still, his desk was a mess. So far Marie hadn't found a way to encourage change. She wouldn't stop trying … she was an optimist and believed the best was yet to come.

My middle name is Marie! (I'm talking about me … Joan Marie Burge!) I'm the one who is well organized and I'm always on the look out for tools and tips that will help me do an even better job of organizing. Of course, I'm no longer an Admin supporting someone else but I think back to the army sergeant accusations and I smile! I could never accomplish all that I do without good systems and organization. I know the image I project works for me. Everyone who interacts with Office Dynamics expects us to be well-organized and lots more (i.e., enthusiastic, capable, cooperative, dependable).

When someone enters your work area:

- Establish contact.
- Sit up straight and lean into conversations.
- Project confidence when you stand – your posture is showing.

THAT ALL IMPORTANT SMILE

The following recommendations are found in Everyday Business Etiquette by Marilyn Pincus. (See page 124.)

- Smile when you are introduced to someone.
- Smile when you are feeling uncomfortable or out of place.
- Smile when you give or receive a compliment.
- A false smile is not a thing of beauty.

- Smiles that last too long invite suspicion.
- Smile when you talk on the telephone. A smile can be heard.

"Stand tall, stand erect. If you look like a leader, then you are going to act like a leader. If you look like you have the ability, then you will act like you have the ability."
—Joan Burge

TIPS:

- Make eye contact when someone (especially a customer) is at your desk.
- Do not read emails while someone is talking to you (in person or on the phone).
- Stand when welcoming someone into your office or as she approaches your desk, if she is a visitor.
- When a male and female are introduced, either may initiate the handshake.
- When making introductions, the higher ranking person is addressed first.
- When you forget someone's name, welcome the person with a handshake and reintroduce yourself. Most of the time, that person will mention his name when he responds.

BUSINESS ETIQUETTE TIPS

1. Don't talk with food or gum in your mouth.
2. During a meeting or when a speaker is presenting, do not read emails or look at your Blackberries, Palm Pilots, etc.
3. Always respond promptly to an RSVP.

4. Avoid personal mannerisms (e.g., tapping your fingers on the desk) and speech habits that annoy others.

5. Accept constructive criticism from your manager with grace and poise.

"Business etiquette is practiced to make people comfortable with one another so that business can prosper."
—Marilyn Pincus

ACTIVITY: SELF ANALYSIS

1. List some qualities about yourself that positively affect how you present yourself.

   _____

   _____

   _____

2. List qualities you want to improve or traits you admire and want to own.

   _____

   _____

   _____

3. How will you implement the improvements listed in #2?

   _____

   _____

   _____

BUSINESS DINING ETIQUETTE
(EXCERPT FROM FIRSTIMPRESSIONMANAGEMENT.COM)

"Many business deals have been finalized over an effective business dinner, but even more may have been bungled by a lack of proper manners while dining. Dinner is a chance for your company to have a face-to-face interaction with other business entities and clients. A lack of professionalism at the table can reflect poorly on your company's reputation.

Proper dining etiquette is an important business tool, and employees trained in the art of dining will exude confidence and class while dining. Critical mistakes in business dining – like discussing business matters at an inappropriate time, holding flatware improperly and inappropriate dinner banter – will leave a bad taste in the mouth of a professional. It is important to represent your company effectively while dining, before mistakes are made and deals are lost."

CUBICLE ETIQUETTE

There's little privacy in today's open-office layout. If you or your *cubicle neighbors* want more privacy, here are a few rules of cubicle etiquette that can help.

- *Do unto others*…. If you don't want people to come barging into your cubicle whenever they want, you shouldn't go into others' cubicles uninvited. Treat a cubicle as you would a private office.
- Avoid using the speaker phone; this is not only difficult for the caller, but is most certainly annoying to co-workers.
- Turn down *your volume*. Most often, co-workers don't really want to hear what you are talking about. Overheard conversations sometimes affect co-workers' concentration, thus negatively affecting their quality of work.

- Be aware of "inappropriate" laughter. Have fun at work, but be conscientious of getting too boisterous with a group of colleagues.

- Keep personal calls discreet. What goes on in your personal life should be private.

- Watch your computer screen. There may be things you are doing on the computer that should be "for your eyes only."

- If you've got something confidential to discuss, go elsewhere. Go out to lunch or head into a conference room. Anywhere but in your cubicle where your neighbor can hear.

- Keep in mind that you work in a glass house. Keep it tidy!

Behave and dress as you would for the job you want to have in the future.
Remember: Professionalism is more than a state of mind – it's a state of being.
Enunciate your words at all times so that you're understood.
Avoid saying anything you might later regret.
Think carefully before presenting an idea.
Use grace and tact to impress others with your professionalism.
Stand or sit straight – not just for good ergonomic posture, but also to convey an alert image.
Be proactive and positive. Professionals seek solutions to newly identified problems.
Consider signing up for etiquette courses or online etiquette newsletters to brush up on the latest professional expectations.
A professional is someone who can do his best work when he doesn't feel like it."
—Alistair Cooke, American journalist and commentator.

VERBAL ABILITY/COMMUNICATIONS

- It's not just what you say but how you say it, the words you use, the clarity of your thinking, being able to express your thoughts and concepts to others. Stop and think about what you want to say—don't just blurt what comes to your mind.
- Learn to communicate effectively and clearly with all people with whom you come in contact.
- Be clear, concise; don't ramble.
- Be aware of what you say and how you say it and your tone of voice.
- Especially important—be tactful.
- Being a great listener is trait a professional possesses.
- Respond to correspondence and do it in a timely fashion.
- Return phone calls, especially if you said you would get back to someone with information.
- Don't *shorthand* speech (e.g., say yeah instead of yes) or use slang.

WRITTEN COMMUNICATIONS

- Respond to written correspondence in a timely fashion.
- The body of your letter should be centered on the page, not too high or too low on the page.
- Tone down your business correspondence. No smiley faces or emoticons in your emails.
- Follow these principles of clear writing:
  - Keep your sentences short. Most readers can take in about 30 words without pausing. The average sentence length should be 17 to 20 words.

- o Use simple language. Everyday, familiar words are more effective than complex words and phrases.
- o Eliminate needless words. Do not call March "the month of March."
- o Use an active voice rather than passive.
- o Personalize your message. Use peoples' names and use personal pronouns.
- o Use short paragraphs, lists, tables, and headings. These techniques open the page with more white space and will make your document more readable.
- o Be sure your information is correct. Check your numbers and facts. Do not use flowery words that overstate your case.
- Sequence paragraphs effectively:

WHEN THE READER WILL BE PLEASED

1. Present positive news in the first sentence.
2. Follow with essential details.
3. Close with a reminder of the main idea or a look to the future.

WHEN THE READER WILL BE DISPLEASED

1. Begin with a pleasant or neutral statement. (The first sentence neither presents bad news nor leads a reader to expect good news.)
2. Present the facts. Give supporting reasons.
3. State the bad news.
4. Convey a pleasant or neutral idea in the closing sentence.

WHEN THE READER WILL BE INTERESTED

1. Present the main idea in the first sentence.

2. Follow with essential details.
3. Close with a reference to the main idea or look to the future.

WHEN THE READER MAY NOT BE INTERESTED

1. Begin with an attention getting sentence designed to make the reader put aside other thoughts and read further.
2. Introduce the product or idea and try to arouse interest.
3. Present evidence of the proposal's validity.
4. Close by encouraging action.

UNDERNEATH IT ALL

The image you project matters! You can have great skills, a good attitude, be a team player and set goals for your career but still be held back because of one or more of the things spotlighted in this chapter. If you want to move ahead, pay attention to these details. I've seen many assistants overlooked for promotions because of the color of their hair, or the way they dressed, or their lack of manners. Mastery of these things gives you *the edge*.

And, there's more …

When I feel good about myself, I feel better about others. And, others feel better about me. I call it "the bounce factor."

When Dave was really sick from September, 2007 to June, 2008, there were many days I didn't care how I looked. Dave's life was the most important thing to me and everything else was unimportant. I didn't put on any makeup, not even lipstick; which I love. I didn't care about how my hair looked or, if I looked tired and drawn. On the days I made some effort and put a little color on my face, fixed my hair and chose my wardrobe with care, I felt better about the day ahead of me. It had to be easier on Dave when I looked *put together*. He then saw the advocate he needed me to be. I interacted with highly-intelligent surgeons and oncologists and wanted them to believe they could tell me anything that was necessary for Dave and me to know. They probably couldn't be as forthcoming with a "Joan" who appeared to be falling apart. While they saw my vulnerable side, they still perceived me to be a capable person. When I opened my mouth to speak, I sounded like a capable person. *I loved hearing myself sound so strong*. The "bounce factor" was at work again. *Look good, sound good; get a rewarding reception from others and that influences you to repeat the process.*

Note: For the last year, I've been providing services for a major employer in Bermuda. The female senior executives are impeccably dressed and groomed. They wear business skirts or pant suits, high heels and carry fine handbags. You can tell at a glance which employees are executives. The way they look is a powerful piece of their trademark!

Welcome to the Executive Team. Getting here wasn't easy but you made it happen! You will simply continue to use all those skills and capabilities that got you to the top … and, you will refine them, as needed, and add to them as you go.

> *"Nobody's a natural. You work to get good and*
> *then work to get better. It's hard to stay on top."*
> —Paul Galico, novelist

FIVE

EARNING YOUR RIGHTFUL PLACE ON THE EXECUTIVE TEAM

JOAN'S STORY #1:

John was my first mentor and the first executive I worked with as a partner. He just about shoved me in front of a mirror to make me see I was a valuable employee and my input was essential to the well-being of the team. I was to attend executive meetings with him and I was expected to contribute. I learned at a young age that I was worthy of being taken seriously; would see myself not as working for a boss, but rather as a partner with my executive – and that I deserved the same respect afforded to any other executive. I wasn't a level beneath. Bravo ... my self-perception was changed forever. If you've never been there—been treated that way, you have to visualize it. Go ahead … see yourself starting on the executive team. For me, it led to all kinds of things. It changed the way I thought – I was not afraid to work hard or make mistakes along the way; try new things and learn. I firmly believe my positive self-perception attracted what followed. I received invitations to participate in special events; conferences and meetings to which other administrative assistants were not invited. I was JG's right hand; his shadow. I was everywhere. He saw me as integral to his success. I was in the 'Inner Circle.'

When he was away from the office and called and asked, "What's going on?" … he didn't expect me to say, "Nothing." I quickly updated him. "We got three calls from people interested in attending the next stockholder's meeting."

I had JG's undivided attention whenever we had our one-on-one meetings. No one was to interrupt us. When I worked with other executives in the future, I expected the same. You have to command their attention.

When the Executive Assistant to TRW's CEO was away from the office for one week, I was the one called upon of all the assistants there to handle that important job. Some people might have thought, "I don't want to do this! After all, it means being away from my work and that wasn't going to be easy." But there were real benefits and I made myself very visible to key people inside and outside the organization.

This attitude influenced my career. I didn't have a lot of JG's in the future, but because of what I learned from him, I knew I could teach others how to change self perceptions and command their rightful places on executive teams.

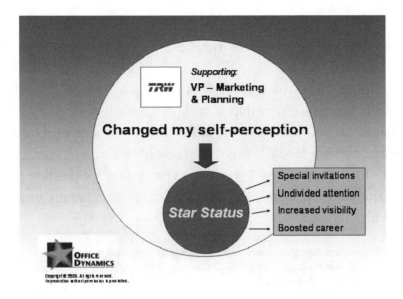

JOAN'S STORY #2:

When I began to work with JR, the General Manager of Steelcase's North Carolina Division, he was accustomed to an *adequate* relationship with his previous assistant. Since they were together for 7 years before I arrived he settled into that avenue of expectations; never anticipating anything different.

I came on board and became an advocate for JR. I wanted to take as much off his plate as I could and make him shine! It took a year to develop the relationship. Because I took the initiative, I earned my executive's respect. I *grew* my position and during the four years I worked with him had a very exciting and challenging job.

I knew partnership-building with JR was a must. He did not know how to do that and never had experienced the benefits of a synergistic partnership with an assistant. I slowly taught him how we should work together. Trust was a big factor in this relationship. He knew he could trust me; that I would not let him down in anything. This does not mean I didn't make some mistakes and had to learn but he knew I was accountable for my actions.

You can teach your executive how to *partner* with you and coach him or her until the partner-relationship is in high gear. In fact, I've devoted an entire chapter for your executive to read so he or she knows how to maximize your time and talents (See Chapter 10 – Dear Manager.)

When the time came and I was able to prove that my position justified a different title and higher pay, JR became an advocate for me and went to corporate for this approval.

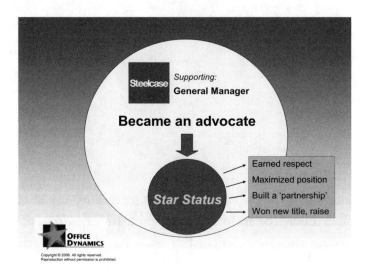

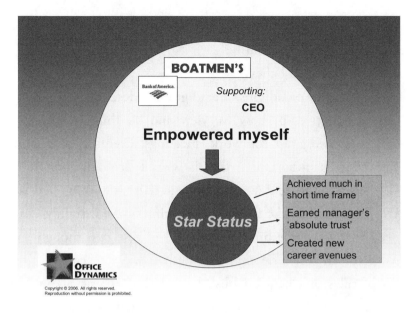

Toward the end of my administrative career, I worked for the CEO of Boatmen's Bank in Memphis, TN. (Here, I achieved a great deal in a short time.) I initiated, created, and implemented Star Achievers™ within the first 3 months of employment. Star Achievers™ was a network and training experience for the company's administrative assistants. (Note: I left Boatmen's after 6 months because my husband made a career move that took us to another city.)

ALL IN GOOD TIME

CD trusted me, gave me the time I needed to create, coordinate, and implement Star Achievers™. The company developed a core of exceptional *Admins* and this opened new doors for me. It led to my second career as Founder and CEO of Office Dynamics.

There is a common thread in these 3 stories.

Can you name it? It starts with an "A" and ends with a "N."

ACTION!

Sometimes assistants say to me, "I wish my executive treated me better or why aren't my ideas taken seriously?"

You achieve what you believe!

Our beliefs are our paradigms. Paradigms are described as

1. Our perspectives or how we view and do things. Example: If I believe showing up for work, meetings, events and even personal gatherings is important – that is what I do! An *Admin* Example: "I've been in the field for 30 years and there is nothing new to learn." OR "I've been in the field 30 years, times have certainly changed. I need to learn something every day." These two thought processes will result in very different outcomes.

2. Set of rules that help establish boundaries. Think about stop signs and imagine what would happen to us if we didn't have stop signs on our roads. There would be chaos. Clearly some paradigms serve us well!

Note: Synonyms for paradigm are: theory, protocol, routines, etiquette, cultures, habits, and customs.

> *"All that we are is the result of what we have thought.*
> *The mind is everything. What we think we become."*
> —Buddha, Hindu Prince, the founder of Buddhism, 563-483
> B.C.

Joel A. Barker (known for many years as "The Paradigm Man") says, "Paradigms can become so deeply rooted that they can become barriers to our abilities to explore new ideas and see new opportunities."

Illustration: In the *Admin* world, an assistant would say, "I'm just an assistant. I can't impact sales or the bottom line." There needs to be a shift in that kind of thinking. While an assistant most likely is not a sales person, she impacts the bottom line by producing quality work, being an excellent representative for the organization, reducing errors, problem solving, troubleshooting, and much more.

"I am just an assistant. I can't impact sales or the bottom line" is nonsense! Step away from it.

Do you harbor long-held beliefs that may be hindering your career?

Since 1990 when I started my business, many high-performing administrative professionals have benefited from adopting the paradigm of a Star Achiever.

According to his Website, Joel Barker's two most quoted phrases are: You can and should shape your own future; because if you don't someone else surely will and – No one will thank you for taking care of the present if you have neglected the future. (Source: http://www.joelbarker.com)

When you perform as a Star Assistant, you become part of the executive team.

How do you accomplish this? I selected my top 9 critical areas; many of which you may never have considered. Well, it's time to *consider*!

NINE TAKE-IT-TO-THE-BANK STEPS

THAT WALK YOU TO YOUR PLACE ON THE EXECUTIVE TEAM

1. Interface Well

<u>Unintentional Interfacing</u> refers to the times people don't purposely focus on making an impression. Another quote from Budda underscores why Unintentional Interfacing can act as either a good friend or a fierce foe:

"Whatever words we utter should be chosen with care for people will hear them and be influenced by them for good or ill."

Remember, you are on stage every day. My time spent at Schering Plough helped lead me to Boatmen's Bank.

Jasmine Freeman's Unintentional Interfacing led her to Office Dynamics. It all began when she attend a training class I offered in Las Vegas. Jasmine wasn't "auditioning" for a job in my company. Quite the contrary, she was taking steps to increase know-how so that she could better serve her Nebraska-based employer. (Read more about this in Chapter 1.)

Unintentional Interfacing is a powerful phenomenon. I'm almost tempted to hand you a Warning Sign ... Handle with Care!

<u>Intentional Interfacing</u>

Look for or create opportunities to interact with management. For example, fill in for the CEO's assistant when she goes on vacation and/or work with Human Resources on special assignments or projects that give you visibility.

2. Think Like an Executive

Q. How can you "think" like an executive when you have never been one?

A. The same way you *imagine* or, *visualize* how beautiful you will be and feel in a gorgeous outfit you admire in a Park Avenue store window. You have never owned such a beautiful outfit but you can still imagine the feeling of possession. Your mind goes there first!

Right Now ...

Go the extra mile.

- We live in a world of mediocrity. There are a small percentage of people who strive to be their best. So if you will just take that extra step or demonstrate extra care, you will stand out.
- Many assistants tell me they don't want to attend their manager's staff meetings because they are too busy! If assistants are to be

taken seriously and considered part of the executive team, then they need to grow and learn to juggle responsibilities as an executive would. Focus on the benefits you will derive from attending these meetings. Many things are discussed in staff meetings that are not in the meeting minutes. These may be little items, but could have significant impact on the department or company. When you attend these meetings, you will be more proactive because you will be keeping your eyes open for anticipated information.

- Preserve your professionalism (and potential).
- Avoid anything that could diminish your professional image or potential.
- Read everything. Be interested in a variety of information. This does not mean you have to read every periodical or magazine from cover to cover. Skim read headlines and quickly grasp news and trends. I highly recommend reading *USA Today*. It is an easy read because of the format and colors. I also suggest reading your partner's trade journals and periodicals.

3. Learn what's important to your executive which may be different than what is important to your colleagues' executive. How do you do this?

Pay attention to details – observe *higher ups'* actions, behaviors, even how they dress.
Listen closely – executive drops clues all the time (with an old assistant I had, I would say, "This is important." And she sometimes ignored what I said.)
When in doubt, ask your executive what is his/her priority.

4. Help Your Executive Look Great

Star Assistants go out of their way to make their partners look good.

- Be an outstanding office liaison (concierge).
- Anticipate (and act on) challenges. Recognize what might make your manager look bad or embarrass him or her. Make it go away!
- Know who's who: a) whom is important to your partner? b) keep your partner informed of any news you read or see about this person or their company.

5. Be a Valued-Added Partner

- Be cognitive. You are more than an order taker and task doer. (If this sounds familiar it is discussed at length in my book, *Become an Inner Circle Assistant*.)
- Understand the scope of your executive's work. This is not the same as what your executive does such as budgeting, hosting meetings, or sales. These tasks don't represent the "big picture" … if you don't fully understand why your manager does what he or she does, find out. If you're ill informed, you won't hear opportunity knocking at the door.
- Demonstrate your worth by taking the initiative and doing little things that have a big impact. For example, when your Manager travels to a place where an industry-related convention is in town – should she attend some sessions? It may be an ideal networking opportunity for her. Find out.

6. Promote Yourself

- Share your positive accomplishments via updates and status reports.

- Stay visible to the *right people* in the company; also known as decision makers.
- Create assignments that bring you in close contact with them (i.e., decision makers).
- When it's necessary to act; act.
- Do something to assist others whenever feasible.
- Always speak optimistically. (Don't operate mouth until brain is in gear!)

7. Think 'You, Inc.'

You work for an employer but you never forget about – *You Inc.*
You Inc., is your primary employer.

- A company has assets. What are your assets? List at least 6.

_____

_____

_____

_____

_____

_____

Showcase your assets at work. Your assets are the things that probably come naturally to you. You may be a great meeting planner, or know how to use PowerPoint to your advantage. You may be well organized, articulate, etc.

- A company also has liabilities. What are yours? List 4 – 6.

_____

_____

_____

_____

_____

An Admin who attended an Office Dynamics workshop listed the following Assets and Liabilities. When you read how she made changes to improve performance, you'll realize why attending an Office Dynamics workshop fit right in to her plan!

ASSETS:

- Enjoy the work I do; strive to do it well
- Organized, quick, and accurate
- Experience in various areas: budgeting strategic planning, reporting, human resources
- Good work ethic
- Good listener

LIABILITIES:

- Lack of confidence
- Put off tasks I don't enjoy
- Let others set my path; put others before me
- Not assertive enough
- Need to develop network

TRANSFORMATION:

- Complete education; spend more time with people who are supportive and positive.
- Improve time management skills by rewarding myself for doing things I don't enjoy.
- Set goals; determine objectives; put role of "others" into perspective.

- Complete intensive assertiveness training.
- Get some training on how to build networks (e.g., buy a good book, attend a specific seminar or, find a mentor who is especially good at this).

8. Use a Creative Approach

If you want to demonstrate your worth to today's fast-paced executive, be creative. Why not create a Career Portfolio? How-to-do-it details appear in an up-coming chapter. Don't miss it and do use it!

9. Map Out a Career Strategy

Today's Star Assistant must align professional goals with the manager's goals, the department's goals, and the company's mission. Remember, *strategy* is the fourth component of Star Achievement. You can have skills for the job, a great attitude and be a team player but, if you do not have a plan to take you where you want to go you won't actualize your professional self.

"If you do not plan where you are going, you will go where everyone else wants you to go!"
—Joan Burge

Imagine that you live in Boston and want to drive to Tucson, Arizona. There are lots of different routes you can take. You probably want the most direct route. If so, you won't travel the ambling scenic route. Clarify specific intentions and do what is necessary to reach your destination.

Getting Into the Executive Suite

Working for a President or CEO

With ambition and training, you can *climb over* the competition.

"My grandfather once told me that there are two kinds of people: those who work and those who take the credit. He told me to try to be in the first group; there was less competition there."
—Indira Gandhi, Indian politician and prime minister, 1917-1984

YOU must always ...

- *Look* professional. Your make-up, jewelry and attire should be impeccable at all times. (Remember, you're on-stage daily until you turn the key at your own front door!)

- Be an active listener in meetings. Look for ways to contribute something of value. Meetings offer a perfect venue to showcase yourself. Active listening results in picking up a potpourri of information enabling you to quickly assess needs or challenges. Your response can be notable. Meeting attendees are looking, listening; waiting to receive directions. At this moment, you're a powerful person!

- Be a *strategical thinker*. This means you don't focus exclusively on the here-and-now, like many do, but instead you focus on long-term pros and cons. Dr. Glenn Pfau, a consultant from Virginia, is an image expert who caused me to take notice of this process: if I do this now – what happens? And, then, what happens? My uncle Ralph, the champion chess player, is a *strategical* thinker. When I observe him over the chess board I can almost "see" *the wheels* turning as he plots and plans what will happen if he makes this move ... or, what happens if instead he makes that move? People who are good at multi-tasking are usually good *strategical* thinkers. I mention this because ... you may already be a *strategical thinker* without realizing it.

- Poise, grace. These two characteristics grab attention and invite applause. You can try to exude poise and grace like royalty does. Close your eyes and picture Crown Princess Mary of Denmark. She is dignified. She is neither too loud nor too soft when she speaks. She stands tall and seems to float across a room rather than walk. She adapts a ballet dancer's carriage as she moves and without speaking a word, she earns the admiration of onlookers.

- Flexible and adaptable. Anyone can work for weeks to prepare for a special occasion and then—suddenly plans change. "Anyone" is likely to moan but not the *Admin* who works in the Executive Suite. She may try to salvage something that wasn't used and apply it elsewhere but she won't focus on disappointment. She doesn't have time! She must focus on making *this* the best of times.

- Tough-skinned. Name an individual who appears not to be hurt by harsh words or unfair criticism. This individual may be said to have tough-skin. Insults, inequities *bounce off* him or her. Of course, this is what on-lookers notice. It isn't necessarily the whole picture. If you could see below the surface you probably would see something completely different ... you might even notice tears. In the Executive Suite, you must be tough-skinned. You need to put your energy into matters at hand. A seasoned Pro doesn't even think about feeling sorry for herself. She acts in a manner that brings credit to her partner, her company and lends dignity to the occasion.

- Take ownership. If you offer an idea – be prepared to support it. If something you work on *goes sour* – be prepared to admit it. People will come to know you as a "stand-up" person. You never slink off to blend in with the wallpaper! You are a force to be reckoned with and someone who can be trusted.

- Inquisitive. *Albert Einstein is quoted as saying, "I have no particular talent. I am merely inquisitive."* Einstein won the Nobel Prize for Physics in 1921. Surely his inquisitive nature served him well. You may not be seeking the Nobel Prize but when you ask questions look for the facts; won't permit anyone or anything lead you astray ... you will also be well served and so will your partner.

- Excellent role model to other *Admins*. Company executives are bound to take note when you're an excellent role model. You may think this is the primary reason to do it but, it's not. The primary reason is to build a strong network of good people. You shall call upon them and they shall call upon you and it becomes a mutually beneficial work-relationship.

- Thirst for knowledge. Good for you, you're inquisitive. You want to know why and why not. When you have a thirst for knowledge you will learn new things. Without this thirst for knowledge you may not know what it is you want to know about! For example, if you don't know that electronic books exist, you won't ask why or how they could be useful to your manager.

- Detailed oriented and see the big picture. Pay attention to details and among other benefits, you won't waste time or money. For example, if your manager wants to host a dinner at a nearby restaurant but the restaurant is not open for dinner ... suggest another restaurant or move ahead choose another restaurant and make reservations. When you *see* the "big picture" ... you know something about why the dinner meeting will take place. If, for example, the company is about to launch a new product and your partner will reveal this to dinner guests ... is it possible to present each guest with a sample? A replica? A get-one-free coupon to be used as soon as it's available? Then again, your knowledge of the big picture may help you rule out that plan altogether. It could be that in light of confidentiality issues – it's too risky to present these materials in a public place.

- High energy. Life in the Executive Suite often proceeds at warp speed. You must be physically and mentally able to keep up or, set the pace! Colin Powell wasn't speaking about *Admins* when he said the following but *this shoe fits* ...

"Look for intelligence and judgment and, most critically, a capacity to anticipate, to see around corners. Also look for loyalty, integrity, a high energy drive, a balanced ego and the
drive to get things done."
—Colin Powell, Secretary of State 2001 – 2004

- Dress neatly. When you are a member of the Executive Team you need to look the part at all times. Even on occasions when the atmosphere is relaxed – neatness counts. Don't consider attendance at a company picnic or an invitation to travel on the company jet as occasions to get too relaxed in terms of wardrobe or grooming. Neatness equates with order. Sloppiness equates with disorder.

"Order is a lovely nymph, the child of Beauty and Wisdom;
her attendants are Comfort, Neatness and Activity;
her abode is the valley of happiness:
she is always to be found when sought for,

> *and never appears so lovely as when contrasted*
> *with her opponent, Disorder."*

—Samuel Johnson, English writer, poet and critic, 1709 – 1784.

I smiled when I first read Mr. Johnson's statement because he is so passionate about the subject. And, I smiled again when I reminded myself, so am I!

- Approachable. In many ways you set yourself apart from other employees. At the same time it's essential that you remain approachable. When you maintain a comfortable balance, you've got the best of both worlds. Easy-to-talk-to, friendly, open-minded; these qualities are apparent to those with whom you interact. In addition to making work hours more pleasant, you are likely to get *the scoop* on things that may benefit your executive in a timely fashion. Again, balance, is the operative word. *How to do this?* It's usually a work in progress.

- Able to take criticism. Criticism can be on-target and when it is; take what you learn and use it. Criticism can be irrelevant, and when it is, let it float on by. It can also be unjust and when it is do a quick calculation. Is this worth my time and energy or should I ignore it? Take note that no matter what kind of criticism you're exposed to, you determine what's to be done. You're in charge!

- Keep your emotions in check. There is a difference between being passionate and getting emotional. And, there is a difference between experiencing a range of emotions and "letting it all hang out" – or, keeping it to yourself. When you toil in the Executive Suite, you don't let it "all hang out." There are great numbers of books and articles that discuss Emotional Intelligence. "Emotional Intelligence at

Work" is a paperback book authored by Hendrie Weisinger, Ph.D. that came up when I looked at www.amazon.com. It is one of hundreds of books on the topic! I mention this to underscore the importance of the topic. Evaluate another person's Emotional Intelligence, and get information to use when you deal with this person. If it's a client, for example, and he berates you when statements arrive late even though you have nothing to do with statements – you've got a finger on the pulse of this client's Emotional Intelligence. Take steps to get his statement to him on time. It doesn't matter that you have nothing to do with the accounting department. The company has an unhappy customer and something must be done about it.

- Evaluate the Emotional Intelligence of your partner and others with whom you interact daily.

UNDERNEATH IT ALL

RESPONSIBILITY – TRUST – CHEMISTRY

These three little words represent much of what is Underneath It All.

I loved working in the executive suite. I recognized it was a great achievement. I learned, first hand, extensive responsibilities came with the territory. I was ready for them. You need to be ready, too. So, tackle challenges, embrace new experiences, keep learning and prepare for the time when you won't feel burdened by responsibilities.

(*Responsibility is the price of greatness.*) *

Trust is of utmost importance. When I leave my office for two weeks, my amazing assistant, Jasmine (i.e., Jasmine Freeman) runs my company! If I couldn't trust her – trust that she will show up, make good decisions, respond to clients and suppliers in a timely fashion and juggle all that is entailed in office management, I could not focus on accomplishing my goals when I'm away. Jasmine helped me build trust by following up and following through. We don't let each other down!

(*Those who trust us educate us.*) *

Chemistry – the reaction of two people to one another – has a lot to do with staying in the executive suite or staying with a particular executive. I never thought about this aspect of "life in the executive suite" until recently. Chief executives who share opinions with me insist that "chemistry" (i.e., personalities, work styles, taste, beliefs, values, ethics, how we approach things and whether we "like" one another) can't be ignored.

"We click or we don't. I shouldn't have to tolerate a partner who irritates me!"

Chemistry may be the missing link in your journey to the executive suite ... it's one thing that is difficult to control. If you're *knocking at the door* but not gaining entry or, if you're already inside the executive suite but you're not happy; think *chemistry*. You may have to search elsewhere to find it. (*Who seeks shall find.*)*

About Responsibility ... Winston Churchill, British author and Prime Minister during World War II. 1874 -1965.

* About Trust ... T. S. Eliot, American born English editor, playwright, poet, 1888-1965.*

* About seeking/finding (e.g., chemistry) ... Sophocles, Classical playwright.*

SIX

THE ANATOMY OF A STRATEGIC PARTNERSHIP

I don't believe there's a more *potentially* satisfying relationship in the business world than that of an administrative professional and his or her executive. I know this from personal experience after spending twenty years in the field working for twelve different executives in five states! Of those twelve, there were only three with whom I had a synergistic relationship or, strategic partnership.

What about the other nine?

We worked well together, but there is a marked difference between the two kinds of relationships. When you have a strategic partnership you are business partners working to achieve the same goals. You are involved in the decision making processes; you make recommendations which are given serious consideration and you're valued as a key business partner.

Of course, there are times when strategic partners disagree.

"A good manager doesn't try to eliminate conflict; he tries to keep it from wasting the energies of his people. If you're the boss and your people fight you openly when they think that you are wrong – that's healthy."

This aphorism is attributed to Robert Townsend. I'm unable to verify "which" Robert Townsend made the observation because there are several well-known people with that name. Still, I offer the observation here because it makes excellent sense to me. (Source:www.thinkexist.com).

There were many times I disagreed with or had a different perspective than my executive. We used those differences to challenge one other and to ensure we made the best decisions.

In fact, only a small percentage of assistants and executives enjoy this very special working relationship.

If you don't, does it mean you should be disappointed or give up?

Certainly not.

You may fall a little short in your attempt to attain this rarified relationship but you can probably experience greater fulfillment when you aim for this *prize*. If you are fortunate to be among the estimated 15% who achieve the ultimate strategic partnership, then good for you!

Janice Seaman has the title Executive Assistant to President and CEO, Mike McAllister, at Humana Inc. Are they strategic partners? Without hesitation, Janice answers … Yes!

"In 1982, I wanted a career change so I enrolled in a local business college. In 1985, I accepted a position with Humana Inc., as an Executive Secretary. Over the next twenty-plus years, I held several positions in the company. Each time I moved, I learned about the segment of the company to which I had transferred. In 2000, I moved into my current position."

"When I reflect on the journey to the Executive Suite, I can tell you that continually learning about our company played a major role ... that; and having the courage to go back to college and receive my degree at age 35."

Joanne Linden, Chief Executive Assistant to Aart de Geus, Chairman & CEO of Synopsys, Inc. happily admits to being party to another strategic partnership.

Here's what Joanne has to say about achieving that goal.

"I enjoyed being a secretary, however, it was an executive's belief in me that pushed me to the next level. He made me realize being a secretary was a career, not just a job. That's when I took control of my career and set goals for where I wanted to be and when I wanted to be there. The first step I took was joining PSI (now IAAP, International Association of Administrative Professionals) where I *networked* with others who felt the same way."

Debbie Gross entered the business world filled with enthusiasm.

"After eight years with the same company, same responsibilities and same 2% increases year upon year in spite of stellar performances, I came to realize that my dreams of being financially secure were dimming. It was up to me to get out of my comfort-zone and seek a career that would offer me growth, challenge and financial rewards. I had more then my share of "we'll keep your resume on file" rejections but, you guessed it; one interview paid off! I salute my strategic partner, John Chambers, CEO, Cisco Systems, Inc. We're still together after seventeen years and I'm *loving* every day that I come to work."

A PENNY FOR YOUR THOUGHTS

If you want more ... it may help you to know that when I was an assistant, I believed I had to enjoy working with my executive. After all, I spent more than forty hours a week with this person which was more time than I shared with anyone else. And if I felt we were not a *good fit*, I quit!

Being miserable each working day (or, even unhappy) was not worth it to me no matter how much I was paid.

WHEN TEAMWORK ISN'T ENOUGH

Do you know how to build a strategic partnership?

A good place to begin is to examine the definition and customize it to fit the people involved. This is easier said than done because people and personalities can be so different. You may want to obtain the dictionary meaning of; partnership. Afterward, *tinker* with your definition. When you finish, everything mentioned below should *ring true*.

- It's a step beyond teamwork; which we have all heard about for years.
- Instead of your executive telling you what to do – you work together from the get-go.
- You *put heads together* to determine how to achieve goals and then, you act.
- You're at liberty to call for one-on-one meetings.
- You discuss the future and strategize steps needed to reach new goals.
- You'll forecast possible road-blocks and consider how to deal with them (i.e., brainstorm what if options).
- And, when the unexpected rears up – you'll confer on what to do about it.

The benefits are far reaching. One that I really like is that you understand the "why" of things. You see precisely how *all* the pieces of the puzzle fit together. You know the big picture and the details. Instead of sitting on the side lines, you're part of the process. You're running the ball down the field and experiencing the glory of the touch down. Others view you as a trusted leader of the management team even if your job title doesn't (yet) spell it out. You're in a strong position to put out fires, to troubleshoot for your partner and this dramatically increases your overall effectiveness.

Here's how I view the anatomy of a strategic partnership:

THE BRAINS:

Use them!

You each use your skills to the optimum in order to be a successful duo. You arrive at the office with all your senses engaged (AKA as a Cognitive Being!). You think through all the steps (i.e., beginning, middle, finale) related to projects, situations, tasks, actions, and relationships. Your partner must be free to focus on work and think at a high level.

Then to keep everything moving and to work in tandem, the following skills operate in high-gear:

- Communication (This includes good listening, initiating purposeful conversation, asking questions, providing feedback, giving details, using the right tools, *visual and verbal*, managing conflicting views, and more!)
- Organizational
- Time and project management
- Preparation Know-How so that meeting time is not wasted
- Cooperation
- Self-management

Resource: I invite you to read my book, *Become an Inner Circle Assistant* (Insight Publishing, Sevierville, TN, 2005) to gain a greater understanding of what it means to be a "cognitive being" and to discover more about the twelve main competency areas you'll want to master to be successful in this role.

THE HEART:

You genuinely care about each other – your successes and happiness. You are aware when something is going on in the other person's personal life that can affect their work. I remember one of my executive's whose wife had melanoma; another executive's wife had a brain tumor. It was my job to express empathy, be a great gatekeeper, proactively take projects off my executive's plate and do anything I could to make his or her life easier. You also are excited when your work partner has a success, his or her child graduates, or spouse got a promotion. It is not a "weird" or "getting personal" thing. It's all on the up and up.

THE SOUL:

This is about using *emotional intelligence* which is not the same as getting emotional. I consider Daniel Goldman the grandfather of EI. (He has written several books on the topic. I have reviewed many of them and you may wish to do the same.) He tells us, "Emotional Intelligence is the ability to sense, understand and effectively apply the power and acumen of emotions as a source of human energy, information, connection and influence." There are four dimensions of EI:

SELF-AWARENESS (MEANS I KNOW ME)

- *As the executive*, I know myself. I know my strengths, weaknesses, habits, peculiarities, what I like and don't like; how I react to certain things, the way I like to work and more.
- *As the assistant*, I know myself. I know my strengths, weaknesses, habits, peculiarities, what I like and don't like; how I react to certain things, the way I like to work and more.

SELF-MANAGEMENT (I MANAGE ME)

- *As the executive*, I stay composed. I manage or channel my emotions, and have self-control. When I'm interacting with my administrative business partner, I do my best to *not explode* but sometimes it happens.
- *As the assistant*, I channel my emotions rather than get emotional. When my executive explodes, I know it is not about me.

SOCIAL AWARENESS (I TRY TO KNOW YOU)

- *As the executive*, I can see my administrative partner is having a rough day today. Maybe something has happened at home. I show sensitivity and try not to overload my partner.
- *As the assistant*, I thank you for the feedback you provide. I know your intention is to help me be the best I can.

SOCIAL SKILL (I ATTEMPT TO FACILITATE SITUATIONS FOR A POSITIVE OUTCOME)

- *As the executive*, I step forward with my administrative partner to use visionary leadership and be a *change catalyst*.
- *As the assistant*, I move in tandem with my executive to influence others to make the necessary changes. I manage conflict resolution and use diplomacy and tact in tough situations. I step forward as a leader as my executive is a leader.

THE ATTITUDE:

This is a cornerstone-piece of the anatomy.

To some extent, it's a cheerleaders' attitude – not shy and retiring and definitely positive.

Assistants and executives, who have great working relationships, have an attitude of, "This strategic partnership is important to my individual success, productivity, and happiness." They believe:

- We *are* a team!
- Together we can tackle anything.
- We accept each other's differences and unique personalities.
- Each of us brings something different to the table.
- Challenges may come our way, but we'll work through them.
- I appreciate your point of view on this.
- You are a part of my success.
- I respect you and admire your work.
- I trust you with all the details.
- We depend on each other to achieve results.
- Today was really rough but tomorrow will be better.
- You did something that upset me today and I need to tell you about it.

It probably sounds like I'm painting a picture of an ideal team and such teams don't exist.

Factoid: they do exist!

Those people face challenges, obstacles, and know what it's like to feel frustrated. But they know how to work around the challenges.

The following self-assessment questionnaire entitled: **Roadblocks to Greater Success** is for you. Go ahead … answer objectively and with honesty. After all, it's for *your eyes only* and you can use what you discover as a means to (perfecting) an end!

1. What are some obstacles that stand in your way to being more productive?

2. What is one thing you would like your executive to (do, stop doing, or do more often)?

3. What strengths do you bring to your role and to your executive?

4. What areas do you need to develop?

A THREE DIMENSIONAL VIEW

Another way to look at the strategic partnership:

1. Your view of yourself (how you think you perform; your strong points and attributes, your weaknesses). This ties back to EI, Self-Awareness. This view is important because you have to decide what skills you need to develop. Leverage your strengths and then grow the other aspects.

2. Your view of what you "*think*" is important to your executive. From where you sit, you form perceptions as to what you think is important in you to your executive.

3. Your executive's view: what's really important to him or her and how would the executive rate you? *Things look different from the other side of the desk.* Sometimes a manager sees strengths the assistant does not see and other times, the executive sees weaknesses. One *Admin* believes he's a great organizer and his manager is thinking, "Oh I wish Joe would attend some classes from 3M on getting organized."

Play to Your Audience

Your executive(s) and potential future managers/executives are your audience. While you need to know your strengths and areas you want to develop, you should <u>want</u> to know what your audience needs. Just a like speakers care about their audiences' needs, objectives, and pleasing them, so it should be for you.

Example: The best executive I ever worked with loved to see information and stats in charts and graphs. So when I presented important information to him, I put it in chart or graph format (even though I disliked them.) I am visual. Even though Jasmine (i.e., Jasmine Freeman) coordinates all my travel, instead of just "telling" me about my options, I want to see it on paper. I also like information to be presented short and to the point! Jasmine being the "star" she is, will give me updates and other information in bullet format.

I have an assignment for you should you choose to be adventurous. Interview your executive and ask the following questions.

1. What five skills do you think are most important for an assistant to be successful in the workplace?

2. What five top attributes or traits do you think a "star" assistant should possess?

3. In all the years you have been in the workplace, can you name three-five attribute, traits, or behaviors you have admired in administrative professionals?

Behaviors of Strategic Partnerships in a Nutshell

- Communicate clearly and regularly.

- Realize you are dependent upon each other to achieve goals.
- Have clear assignments.
- Listen to each other.
- Are comfortable with disagreement.
- Anticipate each other's needs.
- Be organized; have systems in place.
- Respect personality differences.
- Compliment each other on a job well done.
- Act as a sounding board for each other.
- Understand when either person is having a rough day.
- Have personal talk without getting too personal.

UNDERNEATH IT ALL

You may be in a situation where you have to teach your executive how to build a strategic partnership. Out of my three great executive relationships, only one knew how to fully utilize my skills from the beginning. The others had to be educated. They never really had a great assistant and, therefore, really didn't know what to do about building a strategic partnership. Fortunately, they were open to my suggestions, willing to give the relationship time to develop, and enjoyed trying new things.

If you look for a mentor, someone who already enjoys a strategic partnership relationship, she or he may be willing to coach you to the finish line!

Underneath It All, you will be a happier more fulfilled individual when you work for someone who wants to build this partnership with you or someone whose *chemistry* just clicks with yours. You look forward to going to work and doing a great job. If that is not your situation, you have to ask yourself, "Is that okay? Is there still enough to satisfy me in this position so that I don't want to leave it?" Or, "Is it time for me to move on?"

SEVEN

COMMUNICATION: AS IMPORTANT AS EVER

"To effectively communicate, we must realize that we are all different in the way we perceive the world and use this understanding as a guide to our communication with others."
—Anthony Robbins, American motivational speaker, life coach and author, 1960

From the time we awake until the time we go to bed, we exchange information using a variety of tools. We use cell phones, snail-mail, e-mail, instant messaging, face-to-face discussions, satellite conferences, on-line classes, etc.

Communication links our work together. We receive information from someone, we think about what needs to be done with that information, sometimes we add our own two cents to it, and then pass it on – even if it is to a file. If we are not careful with our part of the process we become the weak link and negatively affect the outcome of an event or project. By leaving out just one word the entire meaning of the communication can change.

Star assistants invest considerable time and effort on their communications. This does not mean they're perfect communicators but they realize the impact communications have in the business world and marketplace. I highly encourage you to research this topic more thoroughly and work on being a Star communicator everyday!

Overall benefits of good communication (regardless of the media used) include your ability to:

- deliver the message you really want to send
- generate enthusiasm for your ideas
- handle challenging situations and difficult people with tact
- think on your feet
- make clear, unambiguous statements
- select the best words; strong, weak or *neither*

OFFICE COMMUNICATIONS

STOP... THINK... SELECT

You have so many choices: electronic communications, snail mail, fax, telephone, voice mail or face-to-face communication. *Which one should I use?* It's important to know when to rely on technology and when the "Human Moment" is critical.

Start with the end in mind and ask:

- What information do I wish to impart?

- What do I need from the other person?
- What do I hope will happen as a result of communicating with this person?

Once you spotlight your goal, try to answer the following questions.

Are you:

- Trying to build rapport or gain trust?
- Making an introduction?
- Relaying a message?
- Expressing an idea or thought?
- Informing co-workers of important news?
- Providing data?
- Disclosing confidential information?
- Introducing others to a new idea?

Consider your relationship:

- How long have you known him/her?
- Is he/she a
    - Co-worker?
    - Staff member?
    - High-level executive?
    - Vendor?
    - Business associate?
    - Mentor?
    - Civic figure or industry official?

Here are a few more questions to ask yourself:

- Could the message I'm delivering be misconstrued?
- Could the information I'm communicating be judged hurtful?
- Could I *come across* as being prejudiced or biased?
- Is this bad news for the recipient?

Since an e-mail recipient doesn't see me and can't hear my voice; will she know when I'm joking?

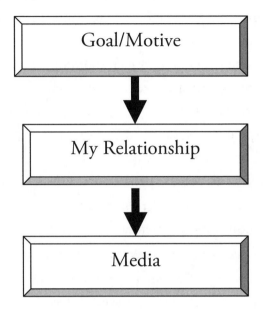

Resource: You can purchase *Real World Communication Strategies That Work* from Office Dynamics. Call 800-STAR-139 or visit our Web site at OfficeDynamics.com.

MAKING THE RIGHT CHOICE

When your goal is to:

- *Build a relationship with a new contact* the preferred mode of contact is: Face-to-face or telephone. E-mail should be your last choice. When you are meeting a new contact, you want her or him to hear your voice and tone. Your sense of humor or business-like manner will be evident. When you're developing a new relationship you want instant rapport. The face-to-face setting is excellent because visibility counts! (NOTE: This presumes you'll present *your very best* self.)

- *Assert needs* the preferred mode of contact is: Face-to-face or, via telephone. Interestingly, some *Admins* debate this choice with me. It seems there's too much room for people to get the wrong impressions when messages are delivered that lack *body language enhancement* or the "personal touch." Numerous research papers from experts at respected universities conclude that what began as small differences between parties ended up in full-blown arguments—all because people communicated via e-mail.
- *Settle differences* the preferred mode of contact is: Face-to-face or via telephone. Never attempt to do this by mail.
- *Confirm a meeting* the preferred mode of contact is: E-mail.
- *Clarify what your executive requested in an e-mail* the preferred mode of contact is: Face-to-face. If necessary, the telephone will suffice. If you want to be "on the record" – e-mail provides you with this opportunity but you may want to use it only to "re-cap" the conversation. Sometimes talking on the telephone or face-to-face saves more time than going back and forth in e-mails. I learned this from a very good teacher – experience! (My own and others, too.)

Choosing the best communication mode is not so easy when you have numerous e-mails to sort through; people at your desk demanding items, a ringing telephone, and you're watching the clock for your executive and putting the finishing touches on her preparations for a business trip that's imminent. It's easy to look at a message in your Inbox and say, "I should call this person, but I don't have time. I'm just going to send an e-mail." The problem is you may end up wasting more time or compromise the good image you enjoy because you didn't select the right media.

E-MAIL STRATEGIES

(Excerpt from *Real World Communications Strategies That Work*,
Co-authored by Joan Burge and adapted for *Underneath It All*.)

(Note to Reader: I've chosen to focus on e-mail in this book because it is the preferred choice and is also creating the most problems. I have written this information in a succinct fashion using bullet points and offering quick tips.)

As much as e-mail provides numerous benefits, it also presents many challenges and has its share of downfalls. For example, here are some ways an e-mail recipient can contribute to a negative communication experience:

- Misinterprets the message. This frequently happens when the sender doesn't provide sufficient information.
- Is offended. Vocal pitch, pace, etc., are missing and the resulting message *comes across* as "harsh."
- Thinks *worst-case scenario* because the sender neglects to "continue the conversation in progress" and introduces something new/different.
- *Burns bridges* with co-workers because of misinterpretation.
- Is less productive because the sender did not give enough details; therefore, the recipient cannot move forward on the project or task until obtaining additional information is forthcoming.

E-mail can also ...
- Make it harder to resolve disputes.
- Take away the opportunity to confirm immediately what the recipient *thought* the sender meant.
- Enhance biased perceptions of the other party.

- Reduce feedback and eliminate social cues that are provided via observing body language.
- Allow for excess negative attention to be focused on statements made.

"We're expecting far too much communication from e-mail," says Quentin Schultze, a professor of communication, arts and sciences, at Calvin College in Grand Rapids, Mich. "There's a tremendous over-reliance on e-mail, which is leading to a lot of confusion, misunderstanding, anger and frustration."

CRAFTING CONSTRUCTIVE E-MAIL CORRESPONDENCE

Communicating with tact is an art. Writing a tactful e-mail is a science that requires purpose and thought. As John Bowie, information engineering executive, says, "E-mail has transformed inter-office communication. Sending messages electronically is painless, instantaneous, and reliable. It's so easy, anyone can do it. And that's the problem."

Star Assistants think carefully about the receiver before sending e-mails. That's critical because without realizing it, we can offend the receiver. The *absent tone* discussed earlier can skew the message leaving it opened to misinterpretation. It's all too easy to misread emotions and to burn bridges with co-workers (and vice versa).

It's not so much what you say as how you say it that's important. A poorly written e-mail will detract from your professional image and could potentially cause conflict or embarrassment. A well-written e-mail will make the receiver more receptive to your message, increase your effectiveness, enhance your professional image and help boost others' respect for you.

EXAMPLE:

Abrupt: "Get me the revisions by Thursday."

Polite: "Please be sure to get the revisions to me by Thursday."

Polite: "I would appreciate having the revisions by Thursday."

SALUTATIONS OR GREETINGS:

The way you greet your reader is important, especially if that person does not know you. It's synonymous to making a first impression.

Appropriate guidelines for greetings:

Formal/Standard greetings:

Dear Mrs. David Burge, Dear Elizabeth, To All Employees

Less formal greeting (for someone you know well):

Hi, Joan! Hello, Joan. Greetings, Joan.

SUBJECT LINES:

The subject line should be an attention-grabber. It's the first "clue" your recipient has as to the importance of the message. People who receive lots of e-mail are tempted to delete messages when information on the subject line isn't compelling. A successful subject line notation pushes your e-mail to center stage (i.e., "open me now").

Congratulate yourself when you write a subject line message that has at least "3" of the following attributes:

- Provocative
- Descriptive
- Specific
- Concise and Clear
- Positive

- Relevant
- Professional (i.e., no nonsense)

Idea: For internal communications only, you can implement action "code" words such as: ACTION, FYI, URGENT, READ.

SIGNATURE LINES:

(Excerpt from *E-mail a Write It Well Guide* by Janis Fischer-Chan)

Set up your preferences so the signature you use most often is the default—the one that's automatically appended to an e-mail unless you specify otherwise. Then set up a few alternate signatures. For example, if your default signature file is very long—your title or position, mailing address, fax number, etc.—create an abbreviated version for e-mail conversations. It's annoying to see a long signature block repeated over and over again in a series of back-and-forth messages.

ACTIVITY: LIST BELOW THE ITEMS THAT SHOULD BE INCLUDED IN THE SIGNATURE, IN ORDER OF PRIORITY.

1. _____

2. _____

3. _____

4. _____

5. _____

Note: The signature line is somewhat subjective because it will vary depending on whether your organization wants a mission statement, tag line, or other pertinent information included.

Bonus Tip: Avoid e-mail "shorthand." (Example: Sincerely, "P" instead of Pamela)

KEEP AN OVERALL PROFESSIONAL IMAGE:

E-mail correspondence tells the recipient something about you. In business, always be as professional as possible, even with people you have known for a long time. You never know if they are going to forward your e-mail. Professionalism is especially important when writing someone for the first time. That will be his or her first impression of you. Yes, even with e-mail, first impressions count!

FORWARDING E-MAIL CAN BE IMPOLITE:

(Excerpt from Las Vegas Review Journal 1/28/08, written by Marshall Loeb)

- Avoid becoming the office spammer. If you've been asked to pass on an e-mail that someone else wrote and you're unsure who the intended recipient is, you might think it's OK to *spam* everyone who might be involved, but it's not. Your coworkers might not know who is supposed to act on the message and thus forward it to even more people, causing companywide confusion.

- Don't spoil your boss's image. If your boss asks you in an e-mail to speak to a coworker about a problem he or she has with that individual, forwarding the message blindly is like setting it in stone. Unless you've requested permission, don't forward anything that was sent solely to you.

- <u>Contain controversy</u>. If you harbor hard feelings toward a coworker, remember that sending or forwarding just one libelous, offensive or obscene remark can result in legal proceedings and multimillion-dollar penalties – for your and your company.

TIPS FOR MANAGING YOUR EXECUTIVE'S E-MAILS:

I could devote a great deal of time to this subject. However, there are many variables. It depends on the agreement you and your executive have in terms of whether you read all his or her e-mails, are permitted to reply to and manage those e-mails, take action, and catalog them. Jasmine and I approach my e-mails in a few different ways depending on if I'm traveling or not; and whether I'm traveling out of the country or, in the USA.

I'd like to encourage you to have a conversation with your executive about this important topic. Determine the best process that works for your executive, implement that process, monitor its effectiveness, tweak if necessary, and then stay with the process. Here are just a few ideas from me and some administrative professionals who graciously share tips with us.

1. Delete e-mails that don't have value.

2. Transfer essential e-mails requesting personal attention from your executive to a separate folder.

3. Set up folders for your executive for non-essential items, such as: To Read

4. In Outlook, use the color flags to:

   - prioritize your executive's (or your own) e-mails (a red flag denotes immediate attention; yellow denotes read at your leisure, and so forth).

- distinguish e-mails for multiple managers you support (one manager's e-mails can be flagged blue, another green, and so forth).

Jasmine created a While You Were Out folder for me and transfers all e-mails to that folder. She opens and manages all of them and indicates whether I have to take follow up action or it's just a FYI. She color codes these for me as well. It certainly makes my life easier when I return from a trip.

ALWAYS BE TACTFUL

"Tact is the unsaid part of what you think."
—Henry Vandyke, American author 1852 – 1933

Your good manners *are showing* when you apply tact. Remember this when you are challenged by atypical communications.

Illustration: Marcy read e-mail for her partner when the woman was out of the country. Together they had decided that Marcy would write a thumbnail comment referencing mail that was important. The rest could wait until her manager returned to the office. One e-mail message was very personal. Her partner's sister discussed sensitive information about their father's deteriorating mental health. Marcy was sorry she had seen it. But, seen it she did. Instead of condensing the information for her executive she passed it along verbatim. She concluded it would demonstrate poor judgment to make any comments. She deliberated on the matter for two seconds. Her good manners (e.g., never be a voyeur or even appear to be one) helped her make the best decision!

"Deliberately create zones of silence in your life where no one can break through to you."
—Brian Tracy

DON'T GO THERE!
THE STARTLING TRUTH (AND RISKS) RELATED TO BUSINESS E-MAILS

February 2008; The American Management Association (AMA) web site:

From e-mail monitoring and Website blocking to phone tapping and GPS tracking, employers increasingly combine technology with policy to manage productivity and minimize litigation, security, and other risks. To motivate compliance with rules and policies, more than one fourth of employers have fired workers for misusing e-mail and nearly one third have fired employees for misusing the Internet.

The 28% of employers who have fired workers for e-mail misuse did so for the following reasons: violation of any company policy (64%); inappropriate or offensive language (62%); excessive personal use (26%); breach of confidentiality rules (22%); other (12%).

The 30% of bosses who have fired workers for Internet misuse cite the following reasons: viewing, downloading, or uploading inappropriate/offensive content (84%); violation of any company policy (48%); excessive personal use (34%); other (9%).

This is another "hot topic" that is not going away. In fact, it will probably grow in prominence as we expand our use of electronic communications. This topic is worthy of an entire series of books. Once again, I'm encouraging you to do further research because it is important. For now, here are the most important items I'd like you to remember.

Remember –

- The company you work for owns the e-mail you write (not you).

- Every time you send an e-mail from work, your company's name is attached to your e-mail address. As a result, your e-mail can put your organization in a good or bad light.

- Improper use of e-mail can increase spam and the risk of viruses. What might be the domino effect if that happened?

- While you may think e-mail recipients delete your messages after reading them, you really don't know – and never will – whether they've been printed, shown to others or forwarded.

- NEVER send confidential information via e-mail.

- Limit or eliminate any personal activity from your company's computer unless you have cleared it with the appropriate personnel.

CONTROL YOUR E-MAIL HABIT

Personally, I love electronic communications. It can end up controlling our lives when we should be controlling it! Here's a summary of the steps you can take to keep e-mail from interrupting your work:

- Turn off your computer's "you've got mail" audio or visual signals.

- Unless you're expecting something important, check your e-mail only at pre-determined times (e.g., 9:00 AM, lunch time, 2:00 PM, 10 minutes before the end of the work day).

- Instead of responding to every message as you read it, "cluster" your responses.

- Don't check e-mail during a meeting.

- If you need to concentrate on something, remove yourself from temptation by working away from your computer or by working offline.

- Focus on the specific e-mail you're responding to or originating.

- Try not to check e-mail just because you're bored.
- E-mail is a business tool. Keep it businesslike.
- Focus on the issue, not the people. Never place blame.
- Read your e-mail before hitting the "send" button.
- Know your company's e-mail culture.

ACTIVITY: ADD YOUR OWN E-MAIL BEST PRACTICES:

_____

_____

_____

Resource: *E-Mail: A Write It Well Guide* by Janis Fisher Chan can be purchased directly from Office Dynamics, Ltd., at OfficeDynamics.com or call 800-STAR-139. Some of the information on this page was adapted from Janis's book.

SMART CELLULAR TELEPHONE USE

The good news is: cellular telephones represent a remarkable convenience – theoretically you're available all the time! The bad news is: you can become one of the growing "techno blunderers" because using cellular telephones improperly is rude and can render you *unwelcome*.

- Cellular telephone technology is good, but not perfect – so always let someone know if you're calling from your cellular telephone in case you're suddenly cut off.
- Never discuss sensitive or confidential information on your cellular telephone. Eavesdropping technology is also advanced.

- When using your telephone in the car, drive carefully! (In some states, only "hands free" cell phone calls are acceptable.

- Be mindful of who is paying for the call. If it's the person you're calling, don't do so without permission.

- Don't use your telephone in crowded areas. Be aware that you may be disturbing others. You demonstrate poor manners if you *broadcast* your conversation.

- Don't answer your cell phone and carry on a discussion in a meeting or when someone is speaking at a conference. If you must take the call, leave the room.

INSTANT MESSAGING & WHAT YOU SHOULD KNOW ABOUT IT RIGHT NOW

Instant Messaging (or IM) is an emerging technology that is used in the office and at home – and sometimes both simultaneously! It gives people the ability to communicate in real time with others in their network – and, like all tech tools, has its upside and downside. It can boost communication or bog down productivity.

In a moment, I'll discuss setting boundaries for use of this technology in the workplace. First, it's appropriate to mention the a, b, c's that are obvious to the Cognitive Being you are (albeit apparently aren't obvious to everyone).

- To prevent "over-use" which readily becomes *abuse*, use IM with a small core of people.

- Stay *on-message*. In other words, don't wander off to discuss the weather, someone's health, etc. Since you only use IM with a small group of people each one knows not to expect pleasantries and won't think you're insensitive since you neglect to inquire about his or her vacation, etc.

- Use IM when it's the best way to communicate. If you need to "think about" something before responding, you may want to exit IM with the promise that you'll send e-mail soon.

- You don't have to respond to an IM. This can seem awkward but it is the best way to let the sender know you're busy.

- Exit quickly. The nature of this technology makes it okay to be "abrupt" … nothing different is expected.

- Like all emerging technologies … you'll find a comfort zone with this one. Feel free to assert yourself, here. Remember, it's an enticing tool but it doesn't have *power over you* … you are in charge!

ESTABLISHING POLICIES FOR IM USAGE

(Quoted from windowsecurity.com/articles)

If your company decides to allow IM, the first step in keeping it under control is to establish usage policies. Some best practices that can keep IM from becoming a bane to your business include:

- IM should not be used as a substitute for e-mail. IM should be used only for questions or announcements that are short and need to be communicated immediately.

- Users should take advantage of IM software features that allow you to present yourself as "busy" or "offline" so they will not be compelled to respond to numerous queries.

- Users should never register with public directories that allow any and everyone to contact you. Instead, users should maintain contact or "buddy" lists of people who can see their online status, and the list should be restricted to legitimate business contacts.

- Users should not be allowed to install their own IM software on company computers. If IM is to be part of your company's communications cadre, the software and its configuration should be standardized and controlled by the IT department as with other business software.

- IM should never be used for confidential communications of any kind unless the IM client supports message encryption.
- If your industry is regulated, you may need to implement an enterprise level IM system that allows you to record all IM communications.

Creating a policy is only the first step. The policy must be disseminated to employees and there must be mechanisms established to enforce them. One enforcement mechanism is stated penalties for violation. Another is to technologically enforce policies and notify everyone you are doing so.

INSTANT MESSAGING ETIQUETTE

(Quoted from pcworld.about.com/news)
- "Knock" before you enter. Inquire if the other party can instant message.
- Be brief. Think short.
- Watch what you write. Whatever you say in instant messages can be saved and sent around.
- Keep it casual. Instant messages are not replacements for serious, face-to-face communications.
- Go easy on jargon.
- Avoid sloppy writing. IM's are meant to be casual, but it's a real turn-off when messages are full of typos.
- Use "away" message alerts.

WORKING TOGETHER AT A DISTANCE

As we travel through the 21st century, we are challenged to work and interact differently. With the changes in office design, technology advancements, flextime, employees working at their homes, and the virtual office, more and more of us have to learn to work well together at a distance. Here are some tips:

- Set up mini-sessions where you can meet face-to-face.
- Write a time map and responsibility sheet.
- Responsibilities must be clear, detailed and specific.
- Give each other regular status updates.
- Take responsibility for your part of the assignment.
- Know when a conference call will be more time-effective than electronic-mail.

Bridging the Age Gap: Business Intelligence,

Generational Truths

Nexters (1980 and later; 70 million)
(Also referred to as the New Kids, Millennials, Gen Y, Echo Boomers, and the Internet Generation)
Core Values: confidence, civic duty, achievement, sociability, morality, diversity, street smarts
Personality: optimistic, prefer collective action, tenacious (confident, determined)

⬆

Gen Xers (1960 – 1980; 70 million)
Core values: diversity, thinking globally, balance, techno-literacy, fun, informality, self-reliance, pragmatism
Personality: risk takers, skeptical, family-oriented, and focused on the job (not on work hours!)

Boomers (1943 – 1960; 73 million)

Core values: optimism, teamwork, personal gratification, health and wellness, personal growth, youth, work, involvement

Personality: driven, soul-searchers, willing to go the extra mile, love-hate relationship with authority

Veterans (1922 – 1943; 52 million)

Core values: dedication, sacrifice, hard work, conformity, law and order, patience, respect for authority, duty before pleasure, adherence to rules, honor

Personality: conformists, conservative, spenders, past-oriented, believe in logic and not magic

They may be different ages, but their values are often the same. Family is the priority value chosen most frequently by people of all generations. According to research by the Center for Creative Leadership, other values important to every generation include integrity, achievement, love, competence, happiness, self-respect, wisdom, balance and responsibility. Just as what's important to them often is the same, so too are their fears. It turns out different generations have similar levels of trust in upper management – namely, not much. "People of all generations, and at all levels, trust the people they work with directly more than they trust their organizations," notes a CLL press release.

Conflict Resolution In A Multi-Generational Workplace

No doubt you've heard that, for the first time in history, we have four generations working side by side – whether they're in offices or machine shops. There are the World War-era "Traditionalists" or "Matures," who are hard-working and loyal; their affluent, influential children, the "Baby Boomers," who value work as the stepping stone to greater comfort and success; the restless, questioning "Generation X," who yearn to make a difference and distinguish themselves in the world; and the youngest group, which has yet to be definitively labeled. They have been called the "Millennials" or "Generation Now," referring to their desire to experience life fully, with no restrictions, right now.

Because each generation has a different view of the value of work in their lives, conflict is bound to happen from time to time. Let's look at two examples that illustrate my point (and I'll bet they'll sound familiar):

Traditionalist Jim cannot understand why Gen Now Kylie won't go the extra mile when work calls for it. In fact, it often seems that Kylie is more interested in socializing and in what the job is offering her than whether she is pulling her weight.

Baby Boomer Kathy gets annoyed whenever Xer Josh challenges her ideas. After all, she's got considerable experience to back up her suggestions! Still, Josh often insists on trying an unproven, different way.

So how can you keep multi-generational conflict to a minimum – and effectively motivate people to work toward a common goal, even if they don't always agree on how to achieve it? Here are a few suggestions:

- **Communicate, communicate, communicate!** Once you've spent a little time learning what motivates the different generations *(see the article-link-reference below)*, try to relate to people by communicating from their perspectives and using their "language."

- **Be aware of the generation gaps.** Knowing these kinds of conflicts are on the rise – and keeping your eye out for them – can be half the battle won.

- **Encourage dialogue on the issue.** For example, get your team together and discuss the different work views and expectations of all four generations. This can help curb conflicts before they even start.

FYI ... HERE'S AN EXCELLENT ARTICLE ON THE TOPIC:

CNN's "Workplace generation gap: Understand differences among colleagues" *http://www.cnn.com/HEALTH/library/WL/00045.html*

The ideas mentioned earlier are proven to work well. But what if a conflict is the "we just don't get along and we're *not* going to get along" type?

Here are some valuable tips that can help you reduce stress *and* achieve even greater career success through skillful conflict resolution:

1. **Avoid assigning blame or passing judgment.** This often escalates a conflict. Instead, keep your comments neutral – focused on the issue at hand and not on what you perceive to be the other person's

shortcomings. (Those can always be addressed later, when emotions aren't running quite as high.)

2. **Hash it out in private.** It's between you and the other party... so keep it that way by moving an emerging conflict into a private space, such as an office or conference room. This will help you both save face and preserve your professional image.

3. **Accept that some things can't (or won't) change.** Many times, conflicts erupt because people want some kind of change to occur in someone else – either in behaviors or actions. But the reality is change often won't happen. Learn to live with what you can and address the issues that really matter.

4. **Watch your tone and inflection.** It's best to keep your voice as calm and low-key as possible. (Tip: If you speak in a lower, quieter voice, the other person is likely to follow suit – and the conflict ratchets down as a result.)

5. **Separate "business" from "personal."** For this technique to work, you've got to keep an open mind and really listen to what the other person is saying, regardless of how you feel about him or her. Is there a mutually agreeable compromise, a solution? In my experience, the answer is almost always yes – if you're willing to look for it.

UNDERNEATH IT ALL

One of the greatest pitfalls of electronic communications is that it denies us what I call *Human Moments*. I do love e-mail and my BlackBerry; don't get me wrong. They are a blessing especially when I'm on the road. Electronic communications keep things moving but *Human Moments* are important. As I travel across the country, going into all types of business establishments – mostly large organizations – I see how much employees are losing the *Human Touch*. I watch employees in their cubicles, and they almost look robotic. They're sitting at computers, *glued* to the screens, sending and reading hundreds of e-mails in one day and Instant Messaging. They are so time compressed to get things done and keep things moving that many don't make time for face-to-face communication. What's interesting, though, is that all these people are still staying connected after work hours!

"We learn about others by interacting over time. Such learning is more successful the more there is ongoing interaction and feedback. If feedback is limited, a person is prevented from developing clarity and confidence." *[Powell and O'Neal, 1976]* While that passage was written more than a quarter century ago, it still holds true. International Speaker and well-known author Dianna Booher delivers a similar message: "People long for human interaction. In such a world of emotional disconnection, there's a growing sense of discontent."

Eight

The Fine Art of Persuasion . . . Sharpen Your Tools

You can't depend *solely* upon past performance success when you focus on persuasion capability and the reason is simple. Things change.

If, for example, you're unfamiliar with today's technology or *vocabulary* you're at a disadvantage. Your colleague talks about the next BlackBerry expected in the market in North America and you look and sound less confident when you don't know any thing about it. Clearly, one of the tools or skills that needs frequent "sharpening" is *what you know*. Never stop learning!

According to Anthony J. D'Angelo, creator of the *Inspiration Book Series* – "Never stop learning; knowledge doubles every fourteen months."

And, there's more. You will size-up your "receiver" before moving ahead. Not everyone is persuaded by the same arguments. And, so it goes ...

Why is it that some assistants make things happen – get what they want where others cannot sell themselves or a great idea? Some master all success components. And, most importantly realize the *whole is greater than the sum of its parts*. When an *Admin* has everything working for her – she has the greatest chance to *persuade* – to get what she wants.

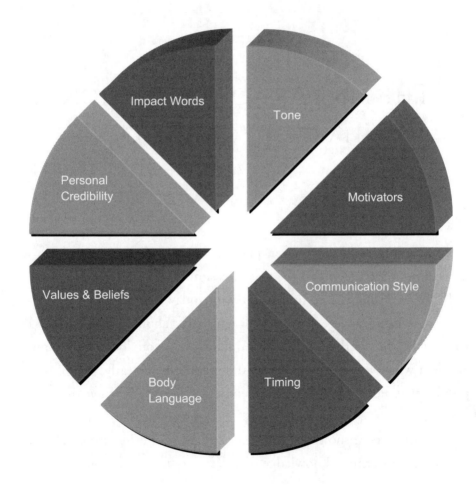

PERSUASION GUIDELINES

1. **Know what you want.** When you work to persuade someone to do something you want to ... make sure you know what you want! If you can't obtain the "whole" will a part (of what you want) suffice? Come to terms with this before you go into persuasion mode. If you don't, you may keep on "pitching" after you've won your *case*. When that happens, you risk losing what you gained.

Illustration: Laura wanted to attend a three day seminar in a nearby city. She showed the seminar brochure to her executive and the woman thought it was a great opportunity.

"It's a shame this is our busy season. If you were gone for three days, I'd be lost without you."

Laura asked for two days and promised she would call in at 4:00 PM on those days for an update. She observed that the recently hired part-time assistant would welcome some extra hours. "Maggie will be right here by your side and I'll check-in with her each afternoon. I can *put out fires* via telephone if necessary. Her executive laughed. "Fires, eh?" Then she surprised Laura by saying okay. Laura didn't try to persuade her that three days would be better until the end of the second day. When she telephoned at 4:00 PM Maggie assured her that everything was okay. So she asked to speak to her partner. "I know how impressed you are with the seminar brochure. It's everything they promised and more! Should I try to get permission to attend the final day?" [Note: The executive could say Yes or, No but – you can see that Laura recognized two days could be valuable. She took them!]

2. **Formulate a clear and accurate plan for persuading others.** Laura countered her executive's concerns by offering a solution; namely, Maggie. The art of persuasion leans heavily on making the other *person feel as though*

he or she is right. You've got to be ready to think on your feet. Laura didn't know what concerns her partner had until she heard her mention – busy season, etc. Laura demonstrated her "cognitive being" status without missing a beat. If she could have anticipated the concerns she might have mentioned getting a "stand-in" for her executive for those three days. All this is conjecture – but conceivably she might have won three day approval up-front had she better anticipated her executive's response.

3. **Consider the buyer's viewpoint.** I often hear assistants say, "My executive will never approve this." As a result, they don't ask for approval! It's important to consider the other person's viewpoint but when you do … be positive.

4. **Show the domino effect, positive or negative.** *Every action has a re-action.* Or, as American author Grace Speare wrote: "For every force, there is a counter force. For every negative there is a positive. For every action there is a reaction. For every cause there is an effect."

When Laura targeted Maggie for additional work, this meant additional pay. The company was expected to pay for seminar attendance too. Laura incurred unusual travel expenses when she traveled to the city. She returned home later than usual so the family ate dinner at a neighborhood restaurant. The costs added up. This is the "domino effect" in action. Laura thought it through at the onset and concluded that a three day investment was do-able and the positive results would make it all worthwhile (i.e., she sharpened skills, Maggie was happy to work additional hours, Laura's partner realized Laura could step-away briefly without ill affect. The family enjoyed dining at a restaurant for three nights in a row. They weren't distracted by telephones, text messaging, etc., and so, they communicated!)

You'll minimize surprises you're not prepared to handle when you consider actions and re-actions.

5. State the benefits of a desired outcome whether for yourself, the receiver, the department, or the organization. "What's in it for me?" is a common question. *Answer it before it is asked* and when you delight people with answers that make them smile, you're likely to get what you want.

6. Watch for bad logic that confuses your audience. If you're well prepared to persuade someone, you have more information than you'll share. If you eagerly explain that you'll return from the seminar with the know-how required to run the latest software but then mention that you can teach these skills to Barbara ... the obvious question is: why are you going to attend when it's Barbara who needs the skills? Of course, the software training is only a small part of what you'll learn. While you don't want to overwhelm anyone with too much information, you want to take care to give sufficient information to prevent confusion. "Two hours on Wednesday morning are devoted to ABC software instruction. I'll be able to share what I learn with Barbara."

7. **Offer options.** You may assume your executive is going to be impressed with the seminar curriculum but, when she isn't you are ready to respond.

"It's important for me to mingle with peers because they often turn into a sounding-board for us when we need recommendations or other input."

"I'm automatically a good-will ambassador for the company. This can result in new business for our company. *Someone tells someone who tells someone* and we don't even know how wide and deep the good news travels." Clearly, this is one kind of option.

Another is your offer to work several Saturday mornings to make up for time missed while attending a seminar. Fact is; there's no end to the options or *alternatives* you will be able to offer to help to make your case.

Another popular option is – the *chocolate or vanilla* one! Not many people would say ... *neither.* "Do you prefer that I attend the seminar in the spring or should I enroll now?" (One way or another you're intent upon going to that seminar!)

8. Keep in mind the format you will use to present your case. So far, we've put the focus on persuading your partner that you absolutely should attend a particular seminar! But, there are many times when your persuasion skills go to work for you and there are other venues or formats to use. For example ... put it in writing ... get a third party involved ... "feed" the person you're planning to persuade a lot of positive information for days leading up to the day *you make your move*.

You say, "You've been reading about the new widget that cuts down on chair fatigue. Are you ready to sign the purchase order for two widgets? We can give them a *test-drive* before considering purchases for the rest of the department."

Or, you want your executive to write a Letter of Recommendation for your son who is applying to college. The college is your executive's Alma Mater and your son is eager to obtain his endorsement. The executive has met your son but before you or your son approach him with a request, you ask your son to obtain a Letter of Introduction from his track coach. This third-party support from a well respected community figure is a plus.

"Martin, my son has assembled these documents (e.g., the Letter of Introduction along with a glowing report card) for your review. He would be honored if you write a Letter of Recommendation for him."

9. Try to gauge your receiver's communication style preference. Some people want details. They want the nitty-gritty. Others want the "bottom line" assessment and that's all. Some people are not *morning people* and you're well advised to make your request in the afternoon. Use what you know about "the receiver" to help you get to YES!

10. **Watch and listen to the receiver.** Tune in to body language. Listen for key words. Top *Admins* do this daily! The information they obtain comes in handy whether they're attempting to persuade or, satisfy or accomplish some other goal. Listen for key words too. When general conversation is replete with negative observations (e.g., *never, forget about it, he's a fool, I don't believe it*) and the atmosphere is charged with negative energy – it's not a good time to approach anyone with your request.

11. **Frame your questions in a way that will generate the answer you want.** Earlier we discussed the *chocolate or vanilla* option. Instead of asking for permission, or for an opinion, ask an executive to make a choice. When you're waiting and waiting for your executive to fill you in on a matter, instead of pleading for her to *make time for you*, ask if Tuesday morning is preferable to Tuesday afternoon apropos your 10 minute tête-à-tête.

Some people ask *funnel questions*. A funnel question begins with lots of information but then is narrowed so the receiver must respond with a YES or NO.

"Jill spent three hours on the telephone with the Burgess people. They were rude to her but she persisted. She asked me if she should call them back next week. I suggested to her that she not call again – do you think I'm right?"

NEGOTIATING WITH MANAGERS

Bargain with your executive. If you can't persuade him or her to *buy-in* on your entire idea, then negotiate. I see this often with assistants who attend my World Class Assistant™ Certificate program in Las Vegas. The attendee will ask her executive to pay the registration fee and they pay their own travel and hotel; or we've even had some attendees invest in the entire package – their registration costs, travel and took vacation days!

When people negotiate typically each gives a little and hopefully (more often than not) you get a lot! You should decide what you're willing to "contribute" before negotiation begins. "I don't have to fly first class!" "I can fly home late in the day and save one night of hotel costs."

Persuasion is a number one topic when it comes to *Admins* who want to attend my classes and seminars. I wrote the following article on the subject which appeared in several publications. It's reprinted here for your review.

GETTING TO "YES"

You know the scenario. You read about a great seminar, workshop, or conference for administrative office professionals. The topics are of interest to you and will help you in your job. You walk into your manager's office to request his or her approval only to hear "no." You walk out. End of story.

Selling your executive on supporting your professional development is a *skill*. It's also known as the art of persuasion. While teaching, coaching, and consulting with thousands of assistants nationwide, I have found that they don't see they have to work at gaining support for training and development. They view it as a yes or no situation. "Yes, I'll get to go" or "My manager will say no." Instead, an assistant needs to view this as, "This is a great program. This will help me become a better assistant and a more valuable employee. How will I sell this to my executive?" You now have your subconscious working to come up with ideas on how to get a "yes" from your executive.

I also hear assistants say, "My executive will never approve this," so they never even present their case to their executive. It's all in positioning your thinking. You have to really believe that you are worth investing in and that you and your executive will both win big with this investment.

I'm providing this advice after being on both sides of the desk. For 20 years I was an assistant and I often had to persuade my executives to let me go to seminars. Since 1990, I've been on the other side of the desk and I now see things as other executives and business owners do. There has to be return on the investment made in an employee. Use the guidelines below to help you sell the seminar or conference to your executive.

WORTH REPEATING

1. You need to continually learn and grow. In today's competitive marketplace and at the pace this profession is changing, if you do not continually enhance your skills, build new ones, and have a strategy for your career, you will get left in the dust.

2. Don't feel guilty about being out of the office to attend something that will make you better, faster, smarter, and sharper.

3. Get your executive to see the long-term payoff. Often executives think about the number of days you will be out of the office. You need to help them see that while you may be gone three or four days, you will gain skills and knowledge that will take you, and them, into the future.

4. Executives travel all over the country. Why shouldn't you? Some assistants tell me they can only attend seminars that take place in their city or state. That is not 21st Century thinking. Assistants should be business partners to their executives, so start acting like a business partner and convince your manager that you should be allowed to travel out of state.

5. I'm sure you receive lots of information on seminars, conferences, and workshops for administrative and executive assistants. You need to be selective. Some things to consider are:

- Who is the speaker? What qualifies this person to speak on the subjects covered?
- If the speaker will discuss how to thrive in your profession, is he or she an expert apropos the administrative profession? Did the speaker ever hold this position?
- What is the value of the program? In other words, what are you getting for your money? The quality of the materials? Any extra events such as a welcome dinner? What meals are included? Of course, the content should always be the most important but when you are comparing one seminar to another and can only attend one, you need to consider these other aspects.
- Is this a lecture or will you be actively involved in the learning process?

6. **Don't give up.** If you really believe this training will help you professionally or even just rejuvenate your enthusiasm about your career, realize it may take three or four attempts to convince your manager. You may have to try different ways or formats to persuade your executive and, remember, timing is important.

Principles of Persuasion

1. Know exactly what you want to accomplish by attending the training or conference.
2. To be a good seller, consider the buyer's viewpoint. Try to put yourself in your executive's position. What key selling points would

be important to your executive? How will your executive benefit when you attend a training session or a seminar?

3. Learn what motivates your executive. Is your executive motivated by ROI (return on investment), the skills you will develop, or you learning from an acclaimed expert in the field?

4. Keep in mind the format you will use to present your case. Try to gauge your receiver's communication style preference. Does your executive prefer information short and to the point or does your executive like details?

5. List the specific topics that will be covered at the seminar or conference and how they tie in to your job or future work.

6. Tie key learning points of the seminar or conference to your professional development plans for the year and goals of your department.

7. Show your executive how what you will learn will help you in specific areas of your job. For example: Let's say one of the topics covered will be learning and understanding communication styles. Tell your executive you will use that information to be a better communicator by tapping into the receiver's style; build rapport with internal and external customers; and complement your executive's and his or her staff's communication styles.

8. If your executive does say no to the training or seminar, sincerely ask your executive why he or she believes this is not a good investment. You may be able to counter that perception.

9. Offer options. Say, "Would you rather I attend the conference in May in California or the seminar in September in Atlanta?"

10. It always helps to let your executive know that you will share what you have learned with other assistants in your organization.

11. Emphasize the benefits of networking with peers and learning from others in the field.

12. Negotiate if necessary. Ask your executive to pay the registration and hotel and you'll pay your airfare. Or, you pay for your hotel stay and ask your executive to pay for registration and airfare. Be creative!

Most of the time assistants tell me they can't attend our programs because of budget cuts. Sometimes it really is a budget issue. Other times, it's just lack of knowing how to sell the program to the executive. Have the courage to go after what you want. That in itself is a learning experience.

INFLUENCE – MORE THAN YOU BARGAINED FOR

When your powers of persuasion are finely-honed, you wield influence because they believe in you. That's an awesome position to hold. So, while you're busy sharpening your tools to achieve goals, keep in mind that you are also establishing yourself as someone whose opinion carries weight.

The scope of your work is poised to expand when your executive begins to know you as an influential person. (This may lead to a new job title and an increase in wages.)

We might conclude that Abraham Lincoln (16th President of the USA) gave the matter of influence serious thought. He wrote, "If once you forfeit the confidence of your fellow-citizens, you can never regain their respect and esteem."

- You may persuade people to "see it your way" because they believe in you (e.g., you're dependable, respected and admired).
- This puts YOU in the enviable position of being a key component of the persuasion equation. No matter how good your powers of persuasion are; if you are an influential person you'll get to YES faster and more often than folks who aren't influential.

You may agree with Mr. Lincoln that once you achieve this status you're wise to handle it with care.

Illustration: Monique conducted herself admirably day in and day out. She was energetic and a good worker. She was always ready to lend a helping hand. She was smart – got the facts straight -- was never late and was ready to assist others. She kept promises. She wasn't wishy-washy and wasn't shy about offering her opinion. People were quick to go along with Monique. "If it's good enough for her, it's good enough for me."

(There are books and articles that discuss the topic of persuasion. None that I have read mention *you or me* and the influence we have on people we wish to persuade based upon our day to day performance. This is one of those nuggets of treasure that is *Underneath It All*. Now, it's yours for the taking!)

Underneath It All

You do have to learn to sell yourself and your ideas. If you want to be more influential in the workplace, accelerate change, lead others, streamline processes and have impact, this is one skill you will have to devote time to developing.

You may find yourself feeling squeamish and anxious at first. As you see the impact this has on your own success, your executive, department, and others, you will feel like a winner!

Others will see you as a person of influence. This can lead to greater career opportunities or community leadership roles.

NINE

TEAMWORK AND PEER POWER

"A group of people is not a team. A team is a group of people with a high degree of interdependence geared toward achievement of a goal or completion of a task."
—Glenn Parker

Post Graduate-level assistants know that forming a variety of team relationships is integral to their success. In this Chapter, we address two specific team relationships.

- The first has to do with forming relationships with all types of people inside and outside the organization. Some examples are *teaming* with new employees, people in your copy center, a service team, 360 feedback team, or job sharing partner.

- The second team relationship is all about creating a collaborative environment with your administrative peers. I call it Peer Power or Strength in Unity.

Glenn Parker said it very well when he said just because a group of people gather, it does not mean they are a team.

FUNCTIONAL OR DYSFUNCTIONAL

Have you ever volunteered for a committee at work or outside of work or, served on a professional committee? A functional team gets things done, makes decisions and takes action. A dysfunctional team talks in circles, typically generates tons of great ideas but disbands without knowing who is doing what. In short, they don't serve a useful purpose.

You cannot achieve your goals or complete certain projects without the assistance of others. People seem to recognize this "wisdom" when they participate in sports but the phenomenon reaches far beyond the field or the court. Famed basketball coach Pat Riley tells us, "Great teamwork is the only way we create the breakthroughs that define our careers."

Even something as simple as getting the staff in the copy center to make sure your work is done on time is important. There is a difference between getting people to support you because you are aggressive and getting them to support you because they like and respect you.

What qualities are required to be a good team player? The list is long, but here are a few. Ask yourself, "What percentage of time over a year do I portray that quality?" Is it 10%? 50%? 80%? Guesstimate as accurately as possible because you're going to rely on that figure as you move forward. Your mission (should you accept it) is to increase your percentage in each area.

_____	Good listener	_____	Good communicator
_____	Patient	_____	Open to new ideas
_____	Accountable	_____	Good attitude

_____	*Walk your talk*	_____	Willing to share information
_____	Follow through	_____	Reliable
_____	Trustworthy	_____	Flexible
_____	Honest	_____	Empathetic
_____	Take the lead	_____	Help others achieve their goals

Below is the short list of benefits that accrue when people work together cohesively:

- shared work load
- learning how to do things differently
- getting feedback on your ideas
- having more fun at work
- building on other's ideas
- more resources
- less time spent on project
- better outcome

THE STAR™ APPROACH TO PARTNERING WITH CO-WORKERS

Q. At my company there is a lack of cooperation and teamwork among staff. What can I do to improve our work atmosphere?"

A. You can play a key role in influencing your co-workers to create a healthy workplace that is filled with trust, respect and cooperation.

The tools you need to create a more professional atmosphere are the four components of my *Star Achievement™* philosophy: skill, attitude, teamwork and strategy.

SKILL ... ENHANCE COMMUNICATION SKILLS.

There is no down-side whatsoever to building communication skills. When you work with others and you have a passion to succeed you can't help but strengthen your communication and consensus-building skills. Remember when you seek someone's input, you "owe" that person feedback regarding outcome. Even if the outcome disappoints you, the fact that you keep others "in the loop" will help you build trust and earn respect.

ATTITUDE ... LEAD THE WAY BY PROJECTING A POSITIVE IMAGE.

What image does management project to staff? Are you and/or your co-workers seen as a positive or negative influence at work? Be aware of the image you project throughout the day. Positive attitudes and actions are contagious. Set the stage by being a positive role model. Look for the opportunity behind every obstacle. Help others to *see* it, too.

TEAMWORK ... BUILD RAPPORT WITH YOUR CO-WORKERS.

Get to know your co-workers on an informal basis. (It's difficult to trust a stranger.) Eat lunch with key staff members who can help create a positive culture. Talk about your concerns and strategies for improving the work environment. Ask for feedback, listen to concerns, discuss barriers and *brainstorm* ideas. Encourage team decision-making and be willing to compromise to resolve issues.

Strategy ... Set Your Goals.

All of the above won't happen without a plan. Map out your strategy. Eating lunch with staffers, keeping people in the communications loop even when you are disappointed with outcomes – these are only two of the rock-solid steps you can take to achieve goals. Take a moment to jot 4 – 6 action steps and implement at least two of them today!

Administrative Peer Power

This is not a "new" idea. When I was an assistant working at TRW in Ohio in the late 70s, I experienced this power. I worked with the Vice President of Marketing & Planning for the Automotive Worldwide Sector. There were 26 people reporting to this Vice President, which included 6 Administrative Assistants and 10 Directors located in Ohio. While we had different personalities, we worked closely and supported one other. Many of us were working mothers with small children who relied on day care services. We found that if we pitched in and helped one another during crunch times, we got the job done faster and no one had to work until 8:00 PM or 9:00 PM or on the weekends. *What is new* is that this concept has become a formal process. Admins worldwide who subscribe to this approach are highly-recognized and rewarded.

Since 1990, I have worked with numerous administrative teams or administrative professional groups in large and small companies in every type of industry. While they may have some different goals and projects, their mission is the same.

Teams on a Mission

Main Purpose: to further the development and skill level of administrative staff in response to the changing office environment.

Their purpose includes: helping their companies achieve goals by identifying continuous improvement opportunities and implementing improved standardized work processes. Their overall goal is to increase efficiency, productivity and accountability thus enhancing the administrative role to management. (*They never could have done it without you!*)

Programs/Projects/Tasks Include:

- Increase opportunities for education, skill building and self-improvement through seminars, classes, programs and a resource library
- Promote dialogue among the company's administrative community
- Increase community volunteer participation
- Identify new resource materials
- Publish internal newsletters or e-zines
- Standardize administrative processes
- Lead projects
- Optimize administrative support personnel
- Form *a lobby* to support the interests of office professionals
- Gain acceptance and recognition for the work they are doing
- Keep up with the rapid changes taking place in their company and the business world as a whole
- Inspire other *Admins* to become role models
- Maintain good relationships with management by hosting quarterly luncheons with senior executives to update them on projects and listen to suggestions/feedback
- Restructure pay grades and titles
- Develop core competencies used for training needs, planning, performance reviews, and cross training

- Manage budgets
- Staff an information hotline
- Help new employees get on board
- Host career development expos
- Provide input for succession planning
- Ensure there is consistence in processes

BENEFITS:

There are too many benefits to mention so I've selected some of my favorites.

- Cost savings to the organization
- Improved performance for themselves and their peers
- Retention in the administrative profession, within their company
- Pay increases or bonuses
- Admin role is elevated
- High-level recognition by Senior Executives and CEO
- Opportunity to travel and present their success at Senior Management Conferences
- Stronger relationships between administrative professionals and management
- Receive funds to support their projects and keep their teams moving forward

While all of this is very exciting and great news for the profession, it takes a plan, desire, time and hard work to mesh into a unit of one. High-performing administrative teams take time to develop into a vibrant force in an organization.

So why are these Admins so successful? First and foremost they recognize that **differences don't have to be liabilities**. They know that each person in that group has strengths *to bring to the table*. In fact, an ideal team would be made up of a mixture of personalities, work experiences, backgrounds, communication styles, and work habits.

THE POWER OF ONE!

These teams *happened* because of one person. One person saw a need and had a vision. That one person had an internal passion—a burning flame. She shared it with another administrative peer and ignited her passion and they shared it . . . before they knew it, it spread like wildfire! What are the qualities and attributes necessary to light the fire in others?

Visionary

Passionate

Committed

Organized

Tactful

Persistent

Polished and Professional

Rapport Builder

Disciplined

And someone who already has 20 things on his/her plate.

ACTIVITY: HOW DO YOU MEASURE UP?
CHECK WHICH BEST APPLIES FOR EACH STATEMENT.

I...	Never	Sometimes	Often	Always
Take ownership of problem situations.	❑	❑	❑	❑
Think rationally and act professionally.	❑	❑	❑	❑
See beyond my own work area; I see the big picture.	❑	❑	❑	❑
Appreciate my peers' unique personalities.	❑	❑	❑	❑
Recognize that others have different work styles than mine and accept that fact.	❑	❑	❑	❑
Offer criticism in a way that is non-threatening and non-offensive.	❑	❑	❑	❑
Have lunch with various *Admins* instead of my same group.	❑	❑	❑	❑
Watch out for hidden anger or resentment as barriers to developing strong relationships with my peers.	❑	❑	❑	❑

IT TAKES COURAGE TO BE THE BEST

Earlier in this book, I wrote about leadership. You may believe the following illustrations spotlight leadership and they do. But, just because we're talking about teams and peer power doesn't mean leadership is neatly tied up in another chapter.

As soon as you distinguish yourself as "different" from those around you relationships change. This "consequence" can be very unsettling if you don't expect it. One of the attendees in a Star Achievement session told me that everyone in her company wears tennis shoes on Casual Fridays. I suggested that she didn't have to dress is such a very casual manner. "You can wear a nice loafer." It was a small thing but she later confided that as soon as she left her tennis shoes at home on Casual Fridays she "felt up a notch." The way you feel influences the way you act. As soon as you take on leadership responsibilities for building or leading teams, get ready to dust off your courage and rely upon it. Some co-workers may be surprised that you're suddenly an assertive person. When you demonstrate that is who you are … it's a little like leaving your tennis shoes at home.

WARNING: I've learned that you can have fear and courage at the same time. When I started speaking I was petrified to get up in front of audiences so my fear was definitely present but I found the courage to get up in front of two hundred people to speak. What is at stake is being the best and assisting others to be the best. By eliminating false expectations the task is easier. So, don't be surprised if people with whom you have worked for ages seem like strangers when you take the reins and do what is necessary to make good things happen.

AT THE STARTING-GATE

If ever there was a time that called for a partnership … for teamwork … it's when you're **at the front end of the team building process.** Find an ally, someone who shares your enthusiasm and is willing to work with you to kick things off! As soon as you do, you automatically *double* chances for success. There are various reasons why this is so and they're discussed in the many books and articles that focus solely on teamwork. I'll give you one reason now: When the going gets tough you can take turns acting as cheerleader. When you're working alone … you've got to be a constant cheerleader and although it's possible, it's much easier when you can share the load.

Henry Ford believed … "Coming together is a beginning. Keeping together is progress. Working together is success." Ford was an American industrialist and pioneer of the assembly-line production method. 1863 - 1947.

PROMOTING TEAMWORK

- Welcome input from others. Respect the ideas of others, just as you would like them to respect yours.
- Remain committed. Problems and frustrations may arise, but don't give up. Be supportive of your colleagues – you need them as much as they need you.
- Trust your colleagues. You and your co-workers are working toward one common goal – a successful business.
- Do your part. Do not let team members down.
- Pay attention to possible stumbling blocks or barriers to the team's progress.
- Inspire enthusiasm.
- Focus on what you can contribute.
- Make things happen by creating something out of nothing.
- Assess the abilities of each team player. Identify strengths and assign tasks or responsibilities based on each person's talents.
- Develop strong communication skills. These should include giving details, providing parameters and deadlines, helping others see the big picture of the project, repeating what you think you heard, and listening.
- Make sure everyone, including you, understands the mission.

RESOLVING TEAM PROBLEMS

No team exists without some problems. No relationship exists without some problems, whether small or large. It is important to the team relationship not to let problems tear down the team and reduce team effectiveness. Turn obstacles into opportunities for growth. Focus on possibilities. Put all your energy into finding solutions and work around the obstacles. Some ways to accomplish this are:

1. Have clear team goals. These can shift as the company, organization or department changes focus.
2. Write an improvement plan. Be specific and review this from time to time. In fact, set a review date when you develop the plan.
3. Clearly identify each person's role. Roles sometimes change or expand with time or to meet organizational needs.
4. Encourage each other. Start discussions, seek information, and make suggestions for reaching goals and resolving differences.
5. Establish guidelines about processes. Determine who handles what part of the process.
6. Be a catalyst for creating change and/or offering solutions and options.

"Administrative Assistants have the ability: with the right support and guidance, this ability can flourish."
—Joan Burge

UNDERNEATH IT ALL

I see a company as a constellation of stars. As each person excels and shines, departments excel and shine and this star-like operation permeates the organization from top to bottom – from bottom to top.

This outcome is highly dependent on placing a value on diversity.

If each employee was a "clone" of the next employee … there would be large chunks of capabilities and experiences missing from the group. One might safely predict that the missing parts, pieces, talents would eventually sink the company.

It behooves you to recognize that it's easy to work with someone who thinks like you or has your work ethic but it can be difficult to accomplish anything when working with a person who isn't like you.

Diversity comes under many headings: religious … ethnic … gender … income … education … generational … skill sets … and more. Look upon differences as assets. To do less is to do a disservice to you and to others.

Apply the many "to-do" recommendations that have been explored in this chapter but underneath it all look upon differences as assets – not liabilities and this insight will free you to soar!

TEN

DEAR MANAGER

Note to Reader: There are more than 30 titles used to represent the administrative profession. That's a tip-off to the *diversity of this role*. For purposes of my book I used the title, Administrative Assistant. This refers to the person who provides administrative support services to you and whom you may consider to be a strategic business partner. It's important to mention, I have used the female gender for ease of communication and because 97% of administrative professionals are female. *For the record …* it is not my intention to exclude male assistants for any reason other than ease of communication. Male administrative professionals will find that *Underneath It All* is as pertinent to them as it is to the women who work in this profession.

Dear Manager,

One of your most valuable assets is your Administrative Assistant.

A Star-assistant handles projects for you so that your work load is effectively reduced, acts as a liaison between you and your staff, helps organize your schedule and acts as a buffer between you and callers who may *unrealistically* demand immediate attention. And, this is just the *proverbial short-list.* Support like this saves valuable time and frees you to devote more time and energy to your core work. You've got everything to gain when you commit to building a strong relationship between yourself and your Administrative Assistant. In the best relationships you are a dynamic duo --- AKA a winning team.

Star manager-assistant teams don't *just happen.* They're created.

These teams bask in the fall-out of synergy! Synergy refers to cooperative action of separate parties so that the total effect is greater than the sum of the effects taken independently. When you experience synergy with your assistant *the right hand knows what the left hand is doing* and vice versa. Your assistant behaves like an *extension of you.* In order for this to occur you play a vital role. Once you tune-in to your responsibilities you're in position to make it possible for your assistant to function at the optimum level.

Star teams reach high levels of achievement (individually and as a team), feel the glory of success, accomplish goals in a timely fashion, and handle any challenges presented to them. I know this for a fact after sitting on both sides of the desk. I was an Administrative Assistant for 20 years prior to becoming Founder and CEO of Office Dynamics in 1990. Office Dynamics specializes in developing assistant and manager relationships.

There is so much information I'd like to share with you, it could easily be the topic for my next book! My goal here, however, is to update you quickly, give you some easy to follow tips, and whet your appetite as to what is possible.

It's my sincere hope that you explore this relationship further with your administrative business partner.

Best of luck!

Joan Burge
Founder and CEO
Office Dynamics, Ltd.

MAXIMIZING THE TIME AND TALENTS OF YOUR ASSISTANT™

PERCEPTIONS

What are your perceptions about the administrative role? Are you aware of all the changes that have taken place in this profession? Do you recognize the value this person can bring to your career and department?

The manner in which you view this role will influence the manner in which you treat this person. If a manager believes the administrative professional is there to take orders and fulfill requests, then that is what usually happens. On the other hand, the manager who sees this person as someone who can make decisions, be a business partner, and confidante, will behave differently and witness a different outcome—*a much better one*!

Your perception applies to how you view the manager/assistant team as well. If you view this as a team that is supposed to get results, share disappointments and successes, strategically plan for the weeks and months ahead, and drive change—*then guess what*? (From this point forward the future looks brighter!)

TIMES HAVE CHANGED

From	To
Message taker	Call initiator and handler
Task completer	Project manager
Problem identifier	Problem solver
Sole contributor	Partner and team player
Follower	Willing to challenge
Communicated to	Competent communicator
Average interpersonal skills	Excellent interpersonal skills
Direction taker	Self-motivator
Typist	Skilled computer user

From	To
Information collector	Researcher/information organizer
Few challenges	More responsibilities and challenges

ASSISTANTS ARE "THE CENTER OF INFLUENCE"

As one CEO of a Fortune 500 Company told me during an interview, "Administrative Assistants are the center of influence. Executives and individuals who work within an organization do not always realize the power and influence an assistant can have."

This same CEO also warned, "Don't mess with the Queen Bee." In other words, an assistant is the eyes and ears for the executive. "She is a flow manager and allocates time. She can be your greatest asset/ally or, if you aren't careful, she can sting you right where it hurts – in your pocket."

- "Today's assistant has more *horsepower* than the organizational chart reflects."
- "When a manager says he sees no difference in his relationship with his assistant vs. the rest of his staff, I ask that manager if he or she is treating the assistant the same, then, as the rest of the staff."
- A good assistant really knows how the office functions and provides support which allows the executive to be more effective.
- Top-notch assistants display a keen desire to work well with peers and other executives.
- This person takes initiative to recommend ideas for making things more efficient.
- Who sets the tone; positive versus negative? You know who!

- Look for the "big cheese" when it comes to first hand know-how apropos the following: *How to reduce cycle time, how to eliminate frustration, and how to break down barriers when it comes to implementing administrative processes.* (Take a look at your Admin … does she look like a big cheese to you?!!!)
- This VIP is also considered to be the channel of communication and the "glue" that keeps esprit de corps on the company's site.

Here are some strategies CEO's use to build good relationships with their assistants. You don't have to be a CEO to apply these to your *assistant relationship*.

- Give her or, him opportunities to act discretely. (Practice makes perfect!)
- Think: Management team. (Treat an assistant as part of the management team.)
- Don't try to correct every little thing an assistant does (i.e., Nix micro-managing!)
- Communication is #1. "My assistant has a need-to-know. She will be as effective as her information allows her to be." Remember: communication delayed is communication denied … do it now!
- Face-to-face communication is important. Body language can't be seen in an e-mail!
- Listen. Search for understanding.
- Include assistant in goal setting sessions.
- Co-develop assistant's career path by fostering professional growth.
- Set realistic deadlines for projects.

Today's assistant is a dynamic, ever changing, part of the management team, makes decisions, takes risks, and participates in staff meetings.

Through an executive's encouragement, sharing of responsibility, information, and willingness to see his or her assistant as a business partner, the assistant will become a more valuable asset.

EXPECTATIONS OF TASKS: TO DO OR NOT TO DO?

In some ways, this is a big dilemma for managers and executives today because the administrative role is so diversified. I am often asked:

- "Can I ask my administrative coordinator to do…?"
- "Joan, would it be appropriate for me to assign this "X" task?"
- "Am I allowed to ask my office coordinator to book my family vacation?"

Since I can't address every question here, I'm giving you a few examples to consider. You've got to start somewhere and I suggest you start by setting boundaries. *Hold that thought until you peruse this next page and we'll return to it.**

How do you determine what tasks to assign to your assistant? Here are some questions to answer:

- Does my assistant have the innate ability/talent?
  List 4 innate talents your assistant possesses:
  1. _____
  2. _____
  3. _____
  4. _____

- Does my assistant have experience in a particular area that I am not yet aware of? (This could be experience the assistant has from past jobs or outside work activities.)

(Community theatre) _____

- What is the long-term savings in terms of time? If you take time today to teach your assistant a task or a project, how much time will it save you over the next 12 months and beyond?

     Example: It takes you 2 hours to teach your assistant how to do a monthly report but it will save you 2 hours x 12 months = 24 hours. That is the long-term savings. What could you be spending your time on that has a bigger impact than that monthly report?

*   Let's return to Expectations of Tasks for a moment. After you've thought about the process privately … invite your assistant to help set boundaries (e.g., which personal tasks would you be able to handle for me? Could I ask you to schedule my automobile for maintenance, buy theatre tickets for me and my spouse?) You don't need to come up with answers all by yourself; you've got a talented assistant standing by to help you. And, that's what it's all about!

I live in Las Vegas, but I don't gamble. I would, however, wager that you're not delegating nearly what you should be delegating. Because of that you're held back from realizing your greatest potential. An administrative business partner can make or break you. That is a fact. They are either increasing your productivity or, slowing you down.

But this is a partnership. So no matter how well trained, educated, or skilled your administrative partner is, if you are not involved in building the partnership, then it won't materialize.

Why aren't you delegating more? Here are some of the typical answers I hear from managers.

- I'm a perfectionist.
- I had a bad past experience with other assistants who worked with me.
- My current assistant has let me down in the past or embarrassed me.
- I'm too busy to think about it.
- I'm too busy to turn it over properly.
- When I provide constructive feedback about a project, my assistant gets defensive.

What can you do? After all, you owe it to yourself and your assistant to leverage her talents.

BE A BETTER COMMUNICATOR, INCLUDING:

- Provide precise details about projects rather than say … "type this."
- Give detailed direction and guidance in the initial phase of a new project or task.
- Explain why certain things are needed—share the big picture.
- Be open and honest, yet tactful.
- Keep your assistant in the "communication loop."

BRING YOUR ASSISTANT UP TO SPEED

Here's what my great managers and senior executives did to bring me up to speed during my 20-year career as an Executive Assistant.

- Took time to explain things; not just hand me a piece of the project.
- Included me in their staff meetings; and not just for taking notes.

- Invited me to attend special meetings, conferences, and business events.

- Expanded one-on-one meetings to be a time of learning.

- Gave me periodicals, correspondence, and resources to read that related to the business and their area of expertise.

- Set high expectations.

- Communicated the big-picture as well as the details.

SCHEDULING ONE-ON-ONE'S

Because of the multiple daily activities in the office, it is important to establish a regularly scheduled time for you and your assistant to meet without interruption. The best time to do this is in the morning. If you wait until the end of the day, it may never happen as things tend to build as the day progresses. Here are some ideas as to what you would discuss.

*	Calendars	*	Telephone Messages
*	Mail	*	Visitors
*	Department Issues	*	Status Updates
*	Upcoming Travel	*	Follow-up Items
*	Training	*	Future projects

BENEFITS:

- Reduces stress.

- Diminishes last-minute chaos.

- Opens lines of communication.

- Facilitates the planning of days and weeks.

- Decreases paperwork buildup.

- Clarifies expectations for both parties.

- Both parties understand the day's priorities.

- *Flags* issues or situations that might arise.
- Makes working together more enjoyable.

MAXIMIZING TOGETHER TIME

1. Prepare for your time together. <u>Each</u> person should arrive with organized notes for discussion. Be sure to put the most important items on top in the event your meeting is cut short. (Suggestion: accumulate these things in a file between meetings.)

2. Don't allow others to interrupt you unless absolutely necessary.

3. Stay focused on the topics being discussed.

4. Bring closure or identify the next step to everything you discuss.

5. Clarify and confirm who is taking on which responsibility.

6. Give each other quick, clear status updates on previously discussed projects. Maybe keep an on going list on your computer between your meetings.

If you just work on the suggestions above, you will see an increase in productivity. Remember, you need to give this time. Initially when you practice new behaviors, they may feel odd or you may feel they're too time-consuming. It won't be that way three, six and nine months from now.

EXCERPT FROM STAR TEAMS ARTICLE
WRITTEN BY JOAN BURGE
PUBLISHED IN *OFFICEPRO* EXECUTIVE EDITION

Are you impressed by assistants who seem to be able to read your mind? Avoid thinking they can! Even the best assistants will fall short of this expectation, because they can't know what you think at all times.

Perhaps you think you're already giving clear directions when, in fact, you've only described the end result you're looking for – not a roadmap on getting there. Most managers give their assistants bits of information and expect them to piece the entire puzzle together. That works for some assistants, but not for all of them. So remember, the more detailed you are about your expectations – including the way you want things done, as well as deadlines – the more likely your assistant will meet them.

Conversely, give assistants the opportunity to express *their* needs and expectations, too. Often, your assistant may simply require additional information. Ask, "Is there anything you need from me?"

Here are additional questions that can help strengthen the work relationship:

1. How do you suggest we work better together so we're more effective and successful in our tasks and careers?

2. What matters most to you in your professional and personal life? (Note: Asking this question will help you understand who your assistant really is, as well as what may motivate outstanding performance.)

3. How can I use my talents and resources to help you become an even more accomplished and helpful assistant?

You may also want to find time to talk about larger issues, such as the office culture or environment, your families and friends, industry trends or news in your line of business, and your own personal and professional goals as well.

Resource: Bring Joan Burge on-site to conduct her exclusive workshop for managers and executives entitled *Maximizing the Time and Talents of Your Assistant.* Call 800-STAR-139 for details and pricing.

I have written UNDERNEATH IT ALL statements at the close of each chapter in this book except for this chapter. I invite you to fill this end-of-chapter segment with steps you can take to get to know your assistant better or to enhance your working relationship.

I'll start it for you. 1, 2, 3 – here we go:

- Have you read any good non-fiction books lately? Is one suitable to loan (or give) to your assistant? If so, jot titles now. If not, why not look for a book you might want to share with your assistant? Read it. Ask her to read it. Discuss it. You'll get to know more about her values, opinions … *what makes her tick.*

- Do you send your assistant off to participate in learning opportunities? Should you? Ask her to research what is available and ask her why she thinks she could benefit from attendance. If no monies are available in the current budget … let her know you'll ask for monies to be set aside for this purpose in the future. You immediately set into motion her interest in locating a worthwhile learning opportunity and leave her secure in the knowledge that you support her growth and advancement. I invite you to visit: OfficeDynamics.com for information.

- What do you know about ergonomic chairs? Find out. Better yet, ask your *Admin* to do it. Do you each have the most comfortable *work stations* you can have? Check an Internet search engine and you'll find lots of information about: increased productivity apropos optimum work station/area. Try the words: *ergonomic chairs for my desk* and you may come up with more than one million citations! Surprised? I was. Work toward making your assistant and yourself more comfortable. Results should be well worth the effort and investment.

(Note: Institute one change every six months and you're on your way!)

The DNA of a Star Assistant™

What are the qualities, attributes, attitudes, and behaviors of Star assistants? Why do certain assistants stand out and shine brighter than others? Are Star assistants created or is it their innate abilities that allow them to be Stars? Are there certain qualities and traits a person needs to be successful working at the top echelons in the company?

Answer: **Stars are born.**

How can you recognize a Star?

Answer: I can tell you how to do it.

After working with and studying administrative professionals for more than 36 years, I can respond with confidence. We have data that supports the theory that *Stars are born.* This isn't to suggest this is the entire story but it's a break-through discovery.

Why should you hire or promote people who don't have the potential to be the very best? And, why should people who are missing essential "components" vie for these positions? These scenarios result in disappointment for all concerned.

I'm preparing to release detailed information about the DNA of a Star Assistant ™ in 2009.

I invite you to stay in touch with us or … let us know how to contact ou. You're welcome to visit OfficeDynamics.com for regular updates.

RESOURCES and WORKPLACE TOOLS™

Purchase from Office Dynamics (Visit OfficeDynamics.com or call 800-STAR-139. Use Coupon Code UIA101 and receive a 20% discount on Joan's workplace tools; 10% discount on Joan's Peers books.)

<u>By Joan Burge:</u>

Become an Inner Circle Assistant book

Real World Communication Strategies that Work book

Remarkable Women book featuring Joan Burge

Juggling Work, Home & Your Personal Life CD

World Class Assistant Part 1 CD

World Class Assistant Parts 2 & 3 CD

Administrative Excellence: 6 Must-Have Skills for Today's "Inner Circle"
Assistants DVD training kit for 'lunch and learns'

Achieving Star Status and Earning Your Rightful Place on the Executive Team DVD training kit for 'lunch and learns'

Monday Motivators™ free e-zine, providing weekly energizing and informative success tips

By Joan's Peers:

E-mail: A Write it Well Guide by Janis Fisher Chan

Attitude is Everything by Jeff Keller

Everyday Business Etiquette by Marilyn Pincus

Casual Power by Sherry Maysonave

The Complete Conference Planner

Other Resources (not available through Office Dynamics:

- *How to Communicate With Power, Diplomacy and Tact* by Dr. Robert A. Tracz
- *Getting Things Done* by Edwin C. Bliss
- *First Things First* by Stephen R. Covey
- *Cutting Paperwork in the Corporate Culture* by Dianna Booher
- *Best Impressions: How to Gain Professionalism, Promotion and Profit* by Dawn Waldrop
- *The Etiquette Advantage in Business* by Peggy Post & Peter Post
- *The Power of Attitude* by Mac Anderson
- *Change Your Attitude: Creating Success One Thought at a Time* by Tom Bay and David Macpherson
- *Yes! Attitude* by Jeffrey Gitomer
- *Effective E-mail Made E-Z* by Verne Meyer, Pat Sebranek, John Van Rys
- *Send: The Essential Guide to Email for Office and Home* by David Shipley & Will Schwalbe
- *People Styles at Work* by Robert Batton
- *Talking From 9 to 5: Women and Men in the Workplace* by Deborah Tanner
- *Quick Teambuilding Activities for Busy Managers: 50 Exercises That Get Results in Just 15 Minutes* by Brian Cole Miller
- *Orchestrating Collaboration at Work* by Arthur Van Gundy
- *Emotional Intelligence: Why It Can Matter More Than IQ* by Daniel Goleman
- *Principles of Self Management* by John C. Maxwell, Ph.D.
- *The Power of Choice: A Guide to Personal & Professional Self Management* by Ted Willey
- *From Panic to Power* by Lucinda Bassett
- *Techno Stress: Coping With Technology @ WORK @ HOME @ PLAY* by Michelle Weil and Larry Rosen
- *The Office Clutter Cure: How to Get Out From Under It All* by Don Aslett
- *Effective Coaching* by M.J. Cook
- *Goal Setting 101: How to Set and Achieve Goals* by Gary Ryan Blair

Post Graduate Level Revelations Lift Assistants to New Heights

I READ JOAN'S BOOK!

Today is _____.
I, _____, finished reading this
valuable book by Joan Burge, founder and CEO, Office Dynamics
and plan to apply the teachings I have read.

I am reminded that engagement is up to me; the quality of work I
produce is my choice; building valuable relationships will help me achieve
my goals; to treasure family and friends as they feed my soul; to give
others the benefit of the doubt as I may not know what is behind what I
see; and to know that all things are possible with commitment, desire,
and the right attitude. The certificate I receive from Office Dynamics
will be a valuable tool to place in my personnel file and career portfolio.
It demonstrates to others that I truly am committed to education and
development.

To receive your official certificate, complete the information below
and mail to: Office Dynamics, 2766 Evening Rock St., Las Vegas, NV
89135.

<u>Please Print:</u>
Name: _____
Co. Name: _____
Address: _____
City: _____ State: _____ Zip: _____
E-mail address: _____

Be sure to visit Joan's blog for more great information at
OfficeDynamics.com!

A HIGH-LEVEL COURSE PRESENTED BY JOAN BURGE

Discount Coupon

You're invited to attend one session at a reduced price. You've demonstrated your interest in becoming a *stellar* administrative professional by reading my book *Underneath It All*. It would be my pleasure to greet you in the workshop setting.

This discount coupon entitles you to a savings of five percent off the current advertised price for the *World Class Assistant ™* high-level certificate program, held in Las Vegas, Nevada.

For workshop details, agenda and registration information, visit my website, OfficeDynamics.com. This certificate may not be used in combination with other offers and has no cash value.

OFFICE DYNAMICS
2766 Evening Rock Street, Las Vegas, NV 89135
800-STAR-139
OfficeDynamics.com
Email: jburge@officedynamics.com

BECOME AN INNER CIRCLE ASSISTANT
ORDER YOUR COPY TODAY!

BECOME AN INNER CIRCLE ASSISTANT is loaded with practical, step-by-step guidance on how to achieve the standards Joan sets for the "next-generation" executive assistant. It is a book of strategy and workplace philosophy that will help administrative professionals become top performers in work and in their careers. The people who support company *movers and shakers* have the opportunity to move into an *Inner Circle*, and this book outlines the steps to get there as well as thrive in the position.

Please print legibly and complete all information in case we have questions and need to contact you.

Name: _____

Company: _____

Address: _____Mail Stop: _____

City: _____State:_____Zip:_____

E-mail: _____

Phone: _____ Fax: _____

Quantity: _____ at $19.95/each **Total Amount of Order:** _____

Payment: ❒Check ❒Credit Card ❒Money Order (payable to Office Dynamics/U.S. Funds Only) ❒Visa ❒MasterCard

Card Number:_____ Exp. Date: ___/___

Signature:_____

US $19.95 + $6.95 S&H,
Canada $24.21 + $8.43 S&H
Nevada residents add 7.5% tax.
For volume discounts or questions, call 800-STAR-139
Published by Insight Publishing,
6x9 perfect bound

To order, fax or mail
this form to:
Office Dynamics
2766 Evening Rock Street
Las Vegas, NV 89135
Fax: 702-360-5356

Dear Reader,

These examples were provided by various administrative professionals along with a form we use. This is not all inclusive by any means. I hope they will be a springboard to your thinking.

Templates and forms save you time and reduce errors or oversight. Check lists are excellent tools to ensure you are not missing a step in a process. I highly encourage you to create your own, especially for tasks or projects you do on a regular basis.

I invite you to visit our OfficeDynamics.com web site and read my blog for additional forms, check lists, and ideas to help you save time and energy! Also, if you have a great tool we can share with other admins, please mail it to our business address or e-mail to me at JBurge@OfficeDynamics.com. Let us know if you want us to include your name.

Sincerely,

Joan Burge

Joan Burge

(Resource: *The Complete Meeting Planner* is an easy-to-follow yet highly-detailed guide designed in a unique workbook format that allows you to customize the contents and add important documents right into the book. The 24 checklists can be used together to plan an entire conference, or you can pick the sections that are relevant to your meeting. Purchase at OfficeDynamics.com or call 800-STAR-139. Use Coupon Code UIA101 and receive a 10% discount.)

Joan Burge

Travel Itinerary for Washington, D.C.

April 22-23, 2008

Flight Confirmation Code: ABC123

Tuesday, April 22, 2008

6:00AM   XYZ Sedan Service – Pick up from home/to airport
7:50AM   United Airlines, flight 000 departs Las Vegas (seat 7D)
3:35PM   Arrive Washington, D.C. (IAD)

Executive Sedan Service will pick you up at the baggage claim area. Driver will have a sign with your name on it. 866-555-5555

Hotel:
Washington Embassy Row, Hotel
1000 Massachusetts
Washington, D.C.
555-555-3555
Confirmation: xxxxxxx

A Conference Center
1111 Connecticut Avenue NW
Washington, D.C.
555-555-4555

Emergency contact:
Jane Smith
555-555-5555 (Office)
555-555-0555 (Business Cell)
555-555-1555 (Home)
555-555-2555 (Personal Cell)

D.C. Weather Snapshot:

Tue Apr 22		Few Showers	**67°/55°**	30 %
Wed Apr 23		AM Clouds / PM Sun	**76°/59°**	20 %
Thu Apr 24		Sunny	**82°/56°**	20 %

Thursday, April 24, 2008

5:00PM   Executive Sedan Service will pick you up at your
meeting site.
Confirmation: 081255

6:55PM   United Airlines, flight 3333 departs Washington,
D.C. (IAD) (seat 7D)

9:04PM   Arrive Las Vegas **XYZ Sedan Service will pick you up.**

(For first time clients, I also include notes about the company,
overview, vision & pertinent information to the current trip.)

Supervisor's Snapshot

Joe Smith
Senior Vice President
Corporate Communications

Wife: Jane Smith
Children: Sara and Jake
Birthday: January 5

Communication Style

Joe's Characteristics:
Empathetic, personal, intuitive.
Likes to be involved in decision-making process.
Enjoys friendly, informal relationships with everyone.
Dislikes telling people unpleasant things; seeks harmony.

How to communicate with Joe:
Be supportive of his opinions and ideas.
Don't hurry the discussion.
Emphasize feelings.
Try to avoid arguments, look for alternative solutions you can both agree on.
Be friendly and personable; don't let him stray from the subject.

Use Joe for:
Assessing the emotional tone of a situation.
Getting others involved.
Generating alternative possibilities and ideas.
Making people feel at ease; stimulating enthusiasm and support.

Management Style

Joe's Characteristics:
Task-oriented, detail-oriented.
Optimistic, a visionary.

Challenges employees to reach their potential.

Prefers structured approach.

Joe's Dislikes:

Taking calls without knowing who is on the line and what they want.

Typos/errors on documents, email, letters, etc.

Poor use of grammar.

Not being informed of calls from senior officers (should he be on the phone or in a meeting.)

Always interrupt and let him know:

Should his wife, Jane, be holding for him.

Should Mr. Chris, Mr. Victor or other senior staff members be holding for him or want to see him.

SAMPLE
CAREER PORTFOLIO

CREATED BY:
TERRI A. HOWELL-MOSBY
EXECUTIVE ASSISTANT
NATIONWIDE INSURANCE
AUGUST, 2008

TABLE OF CONTENTS

- Informational Page
  - Includes 4 x 6 professional photo
  - Current position/department, boss, and service time,
- My Personal Brand
  - Mission Statement
  - Values Statement
  - Personal Philosophies
  - My Plans (12 months, 3 - 5 year, 5 - 10 year)
- Results and Accomplishments
- Learning & Enrichment
- Thank You Notes & Customer Appreciation Notes
- Illustrations of Work
- My Resume
- Subsequent Work
- Community Involvement
- Summary

DATE:

EVENT:

TO BE COMPLETED:

FOLLOW-UP:

NOTES:

Created by Brenda Mason, CPS, CAP

Nationwide Insurance

About the Author

Joan Burge, a renowned author and administrative expert, has been a visionary for administrative training and development since 1990. One of the first to venture into the administrative training industry, she has become an international administrative expert, trainer, author, and consultant. Joan's never-ending quest for providing top-notch educational programs has earned the respect of premier clients like Cisco, Boeing, Humana, Sunoco, Nokia, Procter & Gamble, Rockwell Collins, National Security Agency, Nationwide Insurance, The Children's Hospital of Philadelphia, and Plante & Moran PLLC.

With more than 36 years of experience in the administrative field, training, speaking, consulting, and entrepreneurship, Joan Burge equips administrative assistants, secretaries and office support professionals to move beyond task work to higher-level functions that meet the ever-changing demands of today's workplace. Joan often consults with executives to ensure they are fully utilizing the talents of their assistants, providing insight on ways they can improve their overall working relationships for greater effectiveness and productivity.

Joan Burge is best known for her Star Achievement Series®, a 12-part Certification and Designation (CEAP) training program designed to promote "Star Performance" among administrative, support and front-line staff. She is the creator and host of the Annual Conference for Administrative Excellence™, the World Class Assistant™ Certificate program, and more than 36 customized workshops and seminars for administrative professionals.

She is the author of the groundbreaking book *Become an Inner Circle Assistant* and 3 other books, as well as 15 workbooks. She is the editor of *Monday Motivators*™ weekly e-zine and has been published in more than 100 trade journals. She is a member of the American Society for Training & Development, the National Speakers Association, the Southern Nevada Human Resource Association, and the Las Vegas Chamber of Commerce.

Before starting Office Dynamics, Joan was an administrative professional for 20 years in 12 different companies in 5 states. She worked her way up from receptionist to assisting CEOs, serving in a variety of industries ranging from small businesses to Fortune 500 companies.

Joan Burge...
A Vision of Excellence
A Vision of Change
A Vision for the Next Generation Assistant

2766 Evening Rock Street
Las Vegas, NV 89135
1-800-STAR-139
OfficeDynamics.com